Praise for *Making Every English Lesson Count*

One of the central challenges facing English teachers today is the huge chasm between research and practice. For many, the field of education research is an impenetrable forest that is simply not worth the effort of exploring at a time when workload is already at unmanageable levels. *Making Every English Lesson Count* is an indispensable guide for English teachers that combines important research from a range of fields with practical advice on how to implement it in the classroom. As a researcher, but more importantly as an English teacher, I cannot recommend this book highly enough. Simply put, this is the book I wish I had read in my first year of teaching.

Carl Hendrick, Head of Learning and Research, Wellington College

Andy Tharby has written the best book on English teaching that I have read. Not only is it full of practical wisdom, arresting anecdote and a thorough understanding of the implications of cognitive science for English teachers, it's also couched in elegantly composed prose and is a joy to spend time with. It will bestride the educational world like a colossus.

David Didau, author of *What If Everything You Knew About Education Was Wrong?*

As with his blog, and previous collaboration with Shaun Allison in *Making Every Lesson Count*, Andy Tharby continues to demonstrate his knack of decluttering and demystifying teaching. This time he effectively, effortlessly and succinctly sets his eyes on the English lesson.

Making Every English Lesson Count cuts right down to the quick of English teaching. Tharby painlessly gets straight to the important issues in the classroom and moves us away from the superficial aspects that distract from quality teaching. Using his friendly and approachable style of writing, he guides us through the principles of what a lesson should have and what a teacher can do to ensure that every lesson counts.

Great teaching is about making the unfamiliar familiar and making the complex simple. This book does just that and it is a welcome addition – I really wish I had had it as an NQT.

A perfect gift for an NQT or established teacher of English.

Chris Curtis, Head of English,
Saint John Houghton Catholic Voluntary Academy

This is a fantastic follow-up to *Making Every Lesson Count*, a book that has proved a solid resource for professional learning at all levels of experience.

Andy offers us a manifesto for great teaching of English, informed by research evidence, experience and pragmatism. His style is thought-provoking and insightful, and altogether a pleasure to read.

Making Every English Lesson Count will no doubt be a staple of all English departments, offering a wealth of advice to support the planning of an ambitious curriculum for our students and allowing colleagues to deliberately practice specific strategies in the classroom, with a focus on explicit teaching based on strong subject knowledge.

An advocate for reading and for expanding our students' vocabulary, Andy's enthusiasm is contagious. He has it right when he quotes Ludwig Wittgenstein: "The limits of my language mean the limits of my world." What a fantastic challenge for all English teachers!

I couldn't recommend this book more.

Hélène Galdin-O'Shea, English and media teacher,
research advocate

Andy Tharby is clear from the outset that there are no silver bullets, and no strategies that will work for all English teachers in all classrooms. He stresses the importance of individuality and context, but also recognises that we can learn much from reading and research, from collaborative dialogue with other professionals and from careful reflection on all we learn as a consequence. How can we adapt what others have found to be successful in order to continue to build and strengthen our own practice?

Making Every English Lesson Count is firmly grounded in the principles of challenge, explanation, modelling, practice, questioning and feedback, and considers these elements of effective practice from a subject-specific perspective: offering practical strategies, specific examples and questions to prompt reflection. Tharby encourages the reader to consider how these ideas could be usefully adapted for best effect in their own teaching practice. The book explores, for example, the central place of the text in English teaching; the importance of background knowledge, both in terms of textual content and context and with respect to mastering literary skills; the crucial place of developing our understanding of vocabulary; and the effective use of supporting visual images. Meanwhile, throughout the book, suggestions based on sound underpinning theory about what learning is, and how it happens, are fleshed out with helpful close analysis and annotation of specific literary passages.

Tharby claims, "Great English teachers must live and breathe their subject." *Making Every English Lesson Count* is testament to the fact that Tharby himself is definitely among their number.

Jill Berry, leadership consultant
and author of *Making the Leap*

Making every
English
lesson count

*Six principles to support
great reading and writing*

Andy Tharby

Crown House Publishing Limited
www.crownhouse.co.uk

First published by

Crown House Publishing Limited

Crown Buildings, Bancyfelin, Carmarthen, Wales, SA33 5ND, UK

www.crownhouse.co.uk

and

Crown House Publishing Company LLC

PO Box 2223, Williston, VT 05495, USA

www.crownhousepublishing.com

British Library Cataloguing-in-Publication Data

A catalogue entry for this book is available from the British Library.

Print ISBN 978-178583179-9
Mobi ISBN 978-178583250-5
ePub ISBN 978-178583251-2
ePDF ISBN 978-178583252-9

LCCN 2017939649

Printed and bound in the UK by
TJ International. Padstow, Cornwall

Acknowledgements

This book would not have been possible without the support, guidance and encouragement of my friends, colleagues and family.

I am also grateful to the many wonderful English teachers I have worked with over the years, whose thoughtfulness and expertise have meant that, for over a decade, I have been able to learn something new every day. The ideas in this book belong to you, not me.

Recent years have seen a surge in teachers using social media and blogging platforms to share resources, strategies and education worldviews. Once again, the ideas and insights you have introduced me to shine through this book.

I thank John and Sue Wolstenholme for their generosity in sharing with me their many years of wisdom. I thank Alex Quigley and Caroline Mortlock for their advice and comments on early drafts of this book. And, of course, I thank Shaun Allison for his unwavering belief in me.

Finally, my heartfelt gratitude goes to Donna and George for their patience, love and good humour. Your support has meant the world to me.

Contents

Introduction

Husband and wife John and Sue Wolstenholme were exemplary English teachers whose knowledge and skill transformed the lives of many young people. On retirement, they had clocked up over seventy years of classroom practice between them. Thankfully, their expertise and wisdom have inspired many new teachers to follow in their footsteps. I am fortunate enough to be one of them.

John and Sue had incredibly high expectations of student conduct and behaviour. They were masters of the craft of reading out loud. They were enthusiastic endorsers of reading for pleasure. And they taught with great sensitivity, empathy and attention to detail.

They had their differences too. Sue was very theatrical. You never quite knew what you would find when you walked into her room! She might be roaring from a desktop, transformed into a fervourous and vitriolic Lady Macbeth. Equally, she might be quietly encouraging her students to tease the meaning from an intricate metaphor. On the other hand, John's room was always a sea of calm. Young people would be working hard and working noiselessly. You would often find John stationed behind his beloved overhead projector, conducting a discussion with wonderful deftness and ease.

Two things that I have learnt from John and Sue inform this book.[1] The first is that no two English teachers are completely alike. We each have to carve out our own teaching identity. The second is that great English teachers must live and breathe their subject. If we teach every moment, every lesson and every topic as if it is the most fascinating thing in the world, then our students are more likely to come to believe this too. As John points out, teaching is an act, the classroom our stage.

---

1   John and Sue were kind enough to allow me to interview them before I started writing.

Nevertheless, individuality and passion are paper thin without methods to bolster them. Research suggests that great teaching requires a theory about what learning is and how it happens.[2] That is to say, we must work from a well-rounded conception of how students improve their reading and writing skills, and how our teaching methods support this. The aim of this book is to provide this evidence.

This is a book for new and experienced English teachers alike. It does not pretend to be a magic bullet. It does not claim to have all the answers. However, the ethos, principles and strategies that will be shared are a mixture of the best research evidence available and the timeworn wisdom of expert English teachers, like John and Sue, from across the globe.

We will also return to the six teaching and learning principles that Shaun Allison and I shared in *Making Every Lesson Count*: challenge, explanation, modelling, practice, feedback and questioning.[3]

2   Robert Coe, Cesare Aloisi, Steve Higgins and Lee Elliott Major, *What Makes Great Teaching? Review of the Underpinning Research*. Project Report (London: Sutton Trust, 2014). Available at: http://www.suttontrust.com/wp-content/uploads/2014/10/What-makes-great-teaching-FINAL-4.11.14.pdf, p. 3.

3   Shaun Allison and Andy Tharby, *Making Every Lesson Count: Six Principles to Support Great Teaching and Learning* (Carmarthen: Crown House Publishing, 2015).

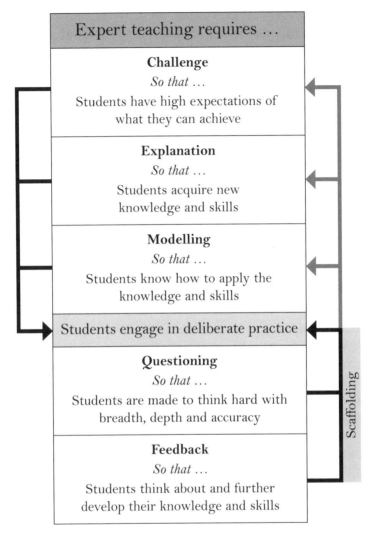

In English lessons, a child learns best when he is *challenged* just outside his comfort zone. The texts he reads should be culturally, linguistically and conceptually rich. He should be immersed in imaginative and academic language, and he should be encouraged to write with ambition and accuracy. However, it is unlikely that he will become an excellent reader or writer by magic. He needs his teacher to *explain* and *model* these highly complex processes with clarity and precision.

Even with great teaching, he will only become a better reader and writer through regular and purposeful *practice*, and he will require *feedback* that will help him to learn from his mistakes and encourage him to think hard and to think critically. Finally, great *questions* will help him to form alternative interpretations and make connections within and between texts.

Now, imagine you were to teach a Year 9 class how to write an analytical essay entitled, 'How does Shakespeare present the character of Romeo to the audience?' You could take the easy option: read one scene, watch the film and hand out an essay plan that tells the class how to write every sentence. This could even produce some sparklingly beautiful essays. Students might appear to show insight and erudition, but sadly this would only be a veneer. It is unlikely that they will have absorbed the play's finer points or learnt how to persevere with an intricate and difficult text.

Real English teaching requires you to take the harder route. The challenge would come from expecting all students – irrespective of ability – to study the entire play. To breathe life into Shakespeare's archaic language, you would need to explain the play's language and themes precisely and memorably. Your class would need to see you model your love for the play and how to grapple with its difficulties, and they would also need practice time to cement comprehension and develop tentative interpretations. Feedback and questioning would then allow you to check understanding and provoke even more thinking.

And that's only the half of it. Once they know the play and have a grasp of Romeo's impulsive character, your students would need to learn how to write an academic essay. Again, high academic challenge would encourage the students to adopt a formal, discursive writing style. Models and examples would make this concrete and achievable. Your feedback and questioning would help them to correct their mistakes and deepen their understanding of how to write in this way.

These six principles should not be considered a lesson plan or a tick-list; in reality, they are members of one body. They sustain each other. Not only do they help you to plan English lessons and schemes of work, but they also help you to respond with spontaneity to the ever-changing and ever-complex needs of your students within lessons.

In recent years, the education establishment has lionised the individual lesson. Indeed, the quality of teaching has been assessed in terms of how successful or unsuccessful a single lesson has been. This has been a mistake. Language learning, for example, is not speedy, linear or logical. It is slow, erratic, associative and cumulative; it does not readily conform to hour-long, bite-size chunks. Research into vocabulary learning, for instance, suggests that young people absorb new words incrementally through multiple exposures to the word in slightly different contexts over time.[4] This is a gradual process that cannot happen in an hour.

Our students, therefore, need teachers who recognise that learning results from artful repetition and consolidation. We must appreciate the interplay and tension between short-term understanding and long-term memory. We must recognise the conceptual and iterative nature of learning. And we must seek to understand the supporting roles of reading, writing, speaking, listening and thinking in this process.

This book argues that English teachers should make use of three pathways to learning: direction, immersion and habit. These interwoven pathways inform each chapter and strategy in this book.

The *direction* pathway covers the huge spectrum of knowledge and concepts that need to be taught and learnt – for example, the spelling of onomatopoeia, the order of events in chapter 1 of *Animal Farm*, the concept of imagery. At

---

4   E. D. Hirsch, *Why Knowledge Matters: Rescuing Our Children from Failed Educational Theories* (Cambridge, MA: Harvard Education Press, 2016), pp. 99–100.

times, these items will be specific to one text or context; at other times, they will be the underpinning concepts that lie at the heart of grammar or literature.

If direction covers the depth and strength of learning, then the *immersion* pathway covers its breadth and diversity. English classrooms should immerse students in language and ideas so that they have every chance of developing new vocabulary and thoughts implicitly and indirectly – through osmosis, if you like. For this to happen, texts and tasks should be chosen with great care. English teaching can have a transformational effect, but only when young people are challenged to read and think beyond the confines of their world. If you choose texts and activities for their entertainment value alone, you are likely to be doing your students – especially those from underprivileged backgrounds – a great disservice.

The last pathway is *habit*. Students will only improve their reading and writing skills if they establish and maintain good working behaviours. This calls for a coherent long-term strategy. First we must decide on the habits we want to inculcate: to independently edit and improve written work? To read each day for pleasure? To elaborate on ideas in full and well-reasoned sentences? To consider alternative viewpoints? Once chosen, we must plan how we will encourage these habits to take root over time until they become automatic in our students.

In each chapter, you will find a number of practical teaching strategies designed to help you to bring the six principles and the three pathways to life. Nevertheless, all schools and classes are different, so it is up to you to refine the strategies to suit the group and topic. After all, you are the expert in your classroom.

Even though this will not be a polemical or theoretical book, it will challenge some prevalent myths in English teaching – such as the belief that English is a 'skills only' subject and the notion that sharing written success criteria is always an effective teaching strategy. The aim of the book is not only to provide practical solutions to perennial problems, but also to inspire reflective thought.

The first four chapters will look at ways to improve reading and the study of literature. In the next four we will turn our attention to teaching writing. Finally, there will be a chapter on how we can improve and speed up the way we give feedback. Each chapter will finish with a series of reflective questions to help you relate the content of the chapter to your classroom practice.

John and Sue Wolstenholme were incredible teachers. If this book proves half as successful in inspiring you as they were in inspiring me, it will be a success.

Let's get going.

Chapter 1

Challenging Reading

Evie and the vicious cycle

Evie is in Year 9 and she does not read books. Neither do her siblings or her parents. Most of Evie's reading – if you can call it that – comes through the social media sites she trawls every evening. Evie's knowledge of the world is shallow and piecemeal: she cannot point to London on a map of the UK; she cannot name the prime minister. Evie feels that she does not need to know these things and that they are irrelevant to her life. If you ask Evie whether she likes reading, her answer is always a resounding "No!"

For many young people, reading comes easily. But for others – like Evie – nature and nurture have been less kind. Sadly, when a child decides that reading is not for her, it becomes very hard to convince her of its joys and virtues. A vicious cycle is unleashed: the less she reads, the further behind she gets, and the further behind she gets, the less accessible her English lessons become.

A possible teaching solution is to choose more appealing texts to read and to plan fun, activity-packed tasks. The theory goes that if Evie becomes engaged by her lessons, she will be more willing to learn. Naturally, there is some truth in this idea – the magical moments of your schooldays most likely inspired you to become a teacher yourself. But even though we hope that Evie will come to love English, teaching her to read with accuracy and confidence must remain the primary goal.

It is also Evie's entitlement to read literature that challenges her to imagine a world beyond the limited confines of her own. It should provoke her to consider times, places, people and ideas that she would not encounter in everyday life. It should open doors to new and fascinating experiences. These doors will not be open at home, only at school. If we deny Evie the opportunity to read challenging literature, we become complicit in a kind of elitism that deems only a certain calibre of child worthy of reading a certain quality of text. This can, unwittingly, perpetuate the social and cultural divides in our country.

Another thorny issue we will address is the 'skills first' approach to reading that has become common in recent years. We often hope that generic skills such as 'language analysis' and 'reading between the lines' will transfer smoothly from one text to the next. Sadly, this is rarely the case. In their excellent book, *Reading Reconsidered*, Doug Lemov, Colleen Driggs and Erica Woolway argue that the skills of reading are not "universally applicable". Instead, they are "applied in a setting, and the details of the setting ... matter immensely".[1]

In other words, you might have taught your students how to analyse the themes of *The Merchant of Venice*, but this does not mean that your students will know how to apply these analytical skills to another text – Emily Brontë's *Wuthering*

---

1   Doug Lemov, Colleen Driggs and Erica Woolway, *Reading Reconsidered: A Practical Guide to Rigorous Literacy Instruction* (San Francisco, CA: Jossey-Bass, 2016), p. 17.

Heights, for instance. The Elizabethan era and the Victorian era were vastly different – as were William Shakespeare and Emily Brontë. To understand and to think critically about a text, a child requires many forms of knowledge: of the writer's life and times; of genre conventions and plot; of language devices and vocabulary; of themes and allusions. In the hope that children will make faster progress, English teachers often make a beeline to teaching generic reading skills before exposing students to the background knowledge they will need to employ these skills. This is a mistake that I made in my first few years of teaching. I call it the 'as-the-crow-flies error'. We cannot think deeply and critically about something unless we have secure 'domain knowledge' to think with.[2] In the study of literary texts, this usually takes two forms: *general* knowledge of literary conventions and *specific* knowledge of the text and its context.

The strategies in this chapter, therefore, have two main aims. They show you how to choose and teach challenging texts. But they also explore how to teach background knowledge more systematically so that students can understand and analyse these challenging texts more successfully.

---

2   See Daniel T. Willingham, Critical Thinking: Why Is It So Hard to Teach? *American Educator* (summer 2007): 8–19. Available at: http://www.aft.org/sites/default/files/periodicals/Crit_Thinking.pdf.

1. Choose Wisely

How should I choose challenging texts to study?

Choosing which text to study can be a tinderbox topic in English department meetings! There are a huge number of factors to consider – from the text's length and its perceived difficulty, to its cultural significance and its musicality when read out loud. Every teacher brings her own set of values and beliefs to the table and, like it or not, we usually have to compromise.

Nevertheless, the most important factor should always be whether the text is challenging enough to take the class out of their comfort zone. These four questions can help you to determine this:

1   Does the text provide enough (or too much) lexical challenge for the age group? Skim through the text. Will it immerse your group in fresh and new vocabulary and expressions? Compare it to another text. Which is the most linguistically rich? If the text is very dense and difficult, will you have enough curriculum time to read it slowly enough for all students to understand it?

2   Does the text allow for participation in the 'conversation of mankind'? In 1962, the philosopher Michael Oakeshott

argued that: "we are the inheritors, neither of an inquiry about ourselves and the world, nor of an accumulating body of information, but of a *conversation*, begun in the primeval forests and extended and made more articulate in the course of centuries".[3] Texts that allow students to step into this conversation of mankind are particularly influential. A class reader should reach out to timeless and universal ideas beyond its immediate setting. Will it provoke your students to think deeply about the human condition – about love or tyranny or honesty – in a way that will enrich discussion and spark debate? Or will you find it hard to get them thinking beyond the text's immediate subject?

3   Does the text introduce literary conventions that induct the students in analytical study? Ideally, each new text should introduce a literary convention or concept that can be taken forward and used to inform and enhance later reading. *Macbeth* introduces tragic structure. Poe's 'The Tell-Tale Heart' introduces the unreliable narrator. Steinbeck's *Of Mice and Men* introduces the foreshadowing technique. Familiarity with all three devices will broaden students' understanding of literature and can be carried forward to the next text. Consider how you can carefully sequence texts so that they tell an evolving story – a meta-story – of literature itself.

4   Does the text provide students with cultural capital and/or useful knowledge? First articulated by Pierre Bourdieu in the 1970s, cultural capital can be defined as the ideas and knowledge that can be drawn on to participate successfully in the intellectual, social and economic life of the land.[4] Shakespeare's plays provide pertinent examples – they are regularly referred to in the media as well as in writing aimed at an educated audience. Some

---

3   Michael Oakeshott, The Voice of Poetry in the Conversation of Mankind, in *Rationalism in Politics and Other Essays* (London: Methuen, 1962), pp. 197–247 at p. 198.

4   Pierre Bourdieu and Jean-Claude Passeron, *Reproduction in Education, Society and Culture*, tr. Richard Nice (London: SAGE, 1977).

texts give unique insights into important historical eras or events – for example, *Journey's End* by R. C. Sherriff teaches us about the physical and psychological effects of trench warfare in the First World War. Other texts introduce students to new cultures and ways of seeing the world – Chimamanda Ngozi Adichie's *Purple Hibiscus*, for instance, is a hard-hitting introduction to post-colonial Africa. At a chaotic children's party that I attended with my son, a fellow parent turned to me and said: "It's all becoming a bit *Lord of the Flies* in here!" Without my knowledge of William Golding's novel, I would have been left flummoxed by his comment.

Once you have answered these questions, you can bring engagement and enjoyment into the mix. Let's say you have whittled your choice down to two novels: *Of Mice and Men* and *To Kill a Mockingbird*. Because each has challenging credentials, you can choose the one that you feel your class will enjoy the most.

Not all English teachers are given the autonomy to choose class readers for themselves, and sometimes you will find yourself in a situation where you have no choice but to teach a text you find simplistic or uninspiring. In this scenario, your only option is to subvert the game. Can you find a route into the 'conversation of mankind' from the text? Could you introduce challenging new vocabulary – feckless, poignant or idyllic – to describe characters, events and settings? Could you expand on the text's themes – perhaps by reading more challenging short stories, poetry or non-fiction alongside? Could you take a simplistic feature, such as the text's narrative voice, and ask the students to consider a twist on it, such as how the text would be different if the third-person omniscient narrator was replaced by a first-person unreliable narrator?

Work by this simple rule of thumb: hard texts should be made easy, and easy texts made hard.

2. Let the Book Do the Teaching

How do I get my students to engage with a challenging book without watering down the content?

In my late teens, I worked in a book warehouse, a monstrous building where pallets of new titles were packed to be shipped across the world. Unwanted and damaged books were also returned to be pulped. One day, I saved a book from a grisly end by slipping it into my bag. It was Vikram Seth's *A Suitable Boy*, a family epic of biblical length set in India. I took it home and gobbled it up, totally enthralled by the way it drew me into a new culture and way of seeing the world. It sparked my fascination with India – a country I have now travelled the length and breadth of several times.

This is why we should never underestimate the great power of books. They can change our students' lives by opening doors into the unusual and unexpected. We should adopt a simple philosophy. The pedagogical methods we use, the activities we plan, the lives and interests of our students, the weather and the time of day should all play subservient roles. The throbbing heart of the English lesson should be the text itself.

Often the best way to engage a student is to ensure that she understands what she is reading. At first, at the factual, obvious level – the who, what, where, why and when. Take the first few pages and chapters of any new text very slowly. If you shoot out of the blocks too quickly, some will become confused and will give up or say that they find the text 'boring'. Given time, their understanding will become more nuanced. Then, characters can be delineated, motives explored, contextual interpretations introduced and fine details closely inspected. Engagement and interest are often a result of this slowly deepening understanding. A ripple that, eventually, becomes a wave.

In truth, we must trust the text to do the engaging for us. Literature is about everything: philosophy, history, science, relationships and the mysterious tensions at the heart of being. Books swamp us with interesting facts: "What's a 'clod', sir?" Yet they also examine eternal truths: "So what have we learnt about the dangers of untrammelled ambition?" The beautiful complexity of the world lies within the greatest literature.

When employed without subtlety, however, some teaching strategies can imply a distrust of literature. Even though games, role plays and flashy slideshows all have their place, trying to engage students through these alone can be a case of not seeing the wood for the trees. A battered, dog-eared copy of *Frankenstein* is an extraordinary tool for teaching and engagement. Use it.

Even so, caution is recommended. Our students must also be encouraged to critique as well as admire. Was Dickens a misogynist? Was Hardy too fatalistic? Did Shakespeare criticise or reinforce the anti-Semitism of his times? Aim, therefore, for a philosophy of cautious admiration. Texts should inspire but they should also be challenged.

3. Plan for Knowledge

How can I ensure that my students fully understand challenging texts?

The first step is always to ensure that you know the text well yourself. Always read a new text in full before teaching it for the first time. This is more important than finding or designing a set of resources. In fact, the best planned lessons and schemes of work usually start from the text and work outwards. As you are reading, make notes and scribble down important questions. Keep a list of the vocabulary words you will need to teach. When you first teach a text you will need these notes. Once you have taught it a few times, detailed explanations and finely honed questions will be at your fingertips.

Some books are huge. Inexperienced teachers can often struggle to decide what to draw their students' attention to and what to tactically ignore. Experienced teachers, however, look for ways, or angles, into the text. Usually, these are based on fundamental literary concepts like characterisation, language and linguistic devices, form and structure, contextual features and authorial intention (see Chapter 4 for more on this). If you are still struggling, consult with colleagues who have taught the text previously. Teacher blogs and online study guides are a great source of help too.

Once your own understanding is in place, the second step is to think backwards from the quality of work your students will ideally produce. Take this paragraph of student writing about Act 1, Scene 2 of *Romeo and Juliet*, when Lord Capulet tells the love-struck Paris that Juliet is not yet "ripe to be a bride":

Lord Capulet reveals his concern about Juliet, his only child, and her future. He explains to Paris that "the earth has swallowed all my hopes but she", which is why he is treating her so carefully. Notice how Shakespeare has personified the 'earth' as a kind of child-eating predator, which reminds the audience just how precious and fragile young life was in Elizabethan times when the infant mortality rate was so high. This line also reminds us of the subordinate position of daughters like Juliet in Shakespeare's time, and how they were controlled by their fathers. No wonder he is careful with Juliet – she a pawn who can be exchanged for his family's future prosperity and reputation.

This paragraph demonstrates a number of reading skills that you would find on a typical exam rubric: the ability to analyse language closely, the ability to consider alternative interpretations and the ability to evaluate a text according to its socio-cultural context. However, these skills are merely the tip of the iceberg. Lying invisibly underneath is deep, secure and well-connected knowledge.

Consider the types of knowledge this student needed before being able to weave everything together:

♦ The storyline of the play.

♦ The literary technique of personification.

- The high infant mortality rates in Shakespeare's time.

- The roles of fathers and daughters in Shakespeare's time.

- The meanings and possible applications of adjectives such as 'precious', 'fragile' and 'subordinate'.

- The spelling of key words (I must have seen Shakespeare spelt at least forty different ways in my career to date!).

- The exact order of the words in the quotation (if this was written in a closed-book exam).

To challenge your students to write like this, you need to prioritise this knowledge in your planning.

Despite planning for this, a common oversight – especially at Key Stage 4 – lies in the overuse of vague and ambivalent exam board rubrics to inform teaching. As David Didau and Nick Rose point out, mark schemes are designed to sample the subject domain, not to determine the content of a lesson.[5] Telling a child to refer to 'alternative interpretations' in their work is only helpful if they already have a number of interpretations at their disposal. Similarly, reminding students to use literary terminology when writing about a GCSE text is only possible if they have studied these features in depth in the preceding years. This is why, when students are first engaging with challenging literary texts, it is far more effective to teach a range of critical interpretations than it is to tell students to make them up.

Consider the following questions before tackling any text or extract:

- What will students need to know about plot, characters and themes?

- What will they need to know about the context the writer was writing in?

- What will they need to know about how the original audience received the text?

---

5   David Didau and Nick Rose, *What Every Teacher Needs to Know About Psychology* [Kindle edn] (Woodbridge: John Catt Educational, 2016), loc. 2282.

- Which vocabulary terms – from or about the text – will they need to know?

- Which literary and grammatical devices will they need to understand?

- What else do I need to find out about the text and its critical reception before I am ready to teach it?

Therefore, assessment criteria should be complemented by content criteria that give students and teachers clear, concise guidance about what needs to be covered, understood and remembered about each text.

Thankfully, English teacher Joe Kirby has created a template for achieving just this – the 'knowledge organiser'. A knowledge organiser is a simple tool that provides clarity for both teachers and students. According to Joe's blog, a good knowledge organiser will "organise all the most vital, useful and powerful knowledge on a single page".[6] For a full play or novel, an A4 knowledge organiser might include several lists of pared down information – perhaps under the headings plot, key quotations, historical context, characterisation and main themes. These central points provide a solid framework around which students can construct and connect their deepening knowledge and understanding of the text. The chief beauty of the knowledge organiser is that it allows for incredible precision and clarity. Students know what they need to learn and retain, and teachers know what they need to teach.

Other teachers and English departments have taken the idea of content organisers even further, giving students and teachers scene-by-scene and chapter-by-chapter advice on exactly what needs to be taught and what needs to be learnt. This approach should not be seen as restrictive. The organisers should specify the *minimum* that students are expected to retain about the text, the essential skeleton. When

---

6   Joe Kirby, Knowledge Organisers, *Pragmatic Education* (28 March 2015). Available at: https://pragmaticreform.wordpress.com/2015/03/28/knowledge-organisers/.

employed with subtlety, this then acts as a springboard for students' personal interpretations and ideas.

Finally, do not feel that teaching knowledge takes away from teaching English. Children with strong general knowledge become strong readers. Helping a child to build his knowledge of the world prepares him to become a better reader – and better readers build their knowledge of the world at a faster rate. Reading expert E. D. Hirsch puts it like this: "To understand language, whether spoken or written, we need to construct a situation model consisting of meanings construed from the implicit words of the text as well as meanings inferred or constructed from relevant background knowledge."[7]

We do not read in a vacuum. Our background knowledge injects life into a text and allows us to make the inferences necessary to comprehend meaning; in fact, it is the invisible ingredient of reading, the yeast in the bread. Without it, understanding becomes very difficult, if not impossible. The skills that we want to see in our students' writing – finely tuned analysis and insightful interpretation – are always underpinned by strong textual and contextual knowledge.

Cognitive psychologist Daniel Willingham puts it pithily: "Teaching content is teaching reading."[8] Knowledge is vital for improving reading, and reading is vital for improving knowledge.

---

7   E. D. Hirsch, *The Knowledge Deficit: Closing the Shocking Education Gap for American Children* (New York: Houghton Mifflin, 2007), p. 39.

8   Daniel Willingham, School Time, Knowledge, and Reading Comprehension, *Daniel Willingham: Science and Education Blog* (7 March 2012). Available at: http://www.danielwillingham.com/daniel-willingham-science-and-education-blog/school-time-knowledge-and-reading-comprehension.

4. Prioritise Vocabulary

How can I make my classroom a vocabulary-rich environment?

Vocabulary knowledge forms the bedrock of reading. In his excellent book, *Building Background Knowledge for Academic Achievement*, Robert Marzano describes words as "tags or labels for our packets of knowledge".[9] A single word is a complete concept that forms a gateway to our storehouse of knowledge on a topic – known as a schema. When we hear the word 'regicide', we immediately recall Macbeth's murder of Duncan – accompanied, perhaps, by a chilling echo of the words "Macbeth doth murder sleep". The word prises open our schema of the play and helps us to connect it with gruesome events from world history.

A wide vocabulary not only helps students to comprehend a text, but it also helps them to make precise and perceptive interpretations and inferences. Cast your eye over these sentences taken from Charles Dickens' *A Christmas Carol*:

Oh! But he was a tight-fisted hand at the grindstone, Scrooge! a squeezing, wrenching, grasping, scraping, clutching, covetous old sinner! Hard and sharp as flint, from which no steel had

---

9   Robert J. Marzano, *Building Background Knowledge for Academic Achievement: Research on What Works in Schools* (Alexandria, VA: Association for Supervision and Curriculum Development, 2004), p. 33.

ever struck out generous fire; secret, and self-contained, and solitary as an oyster.

Even basic comprehension of this passage relies on a huge amount of background knowledge: what a grindstone is; what wrenching, covetous and solitary mean; how flint and steel are combined to make fire; how an oyster hides itself away from the world in its impenetrable shell. Then, of course, students need an extensive vocabulary to be able to comment on this. Scrooge is miserly; Scrooge is misanthropic. They also need secure understanding of literary devices such as metaphor, simile and hyperbole. In other words, the kind of comprehension and analysis expected at GCSE level relies on a huge amount of vocabulary knowledge.

Bringing Words to Life by Isabel Beck, Margaret McKeown and Linda Kucan is a research-informed book that critiques common vocabulary teaching strategies, like getting students to look words up in a dictionary or to work out the meaning from contextual clues.[10] Beck et al. argue instead for a coherent and direct approach to vocabulary teaching. I have summarised their advice below:

◆ Words should be taught in context, not selected randomly – for example, teach the word 'impulsive' in relation to Romeo's behaviour rather than as a word plucked out of the sky.

◆ Words should be introduced through student-friendly explanations rather than dictionary-style definitions – for example, if someone is impulsive, it means that they act on instinct, without thinking decisions through. If you worked for an entire year to save money for a car and then suddenly decided to spend it all on an outfit instead, that would be an impulsive purchase.

---

10 Isabel L. Beck, Margaret G. McKeown and Linda Kucan, *Bringing Words to Life: Robust Vocabulary Instruction* (New York: Guilford Press, 2002).

- Students need to see how words work in multiple contexts – for example, teacher and/or students could describe moments in their lives when they have behaved impulsively, or perhaps the class could consider the differences between an impulsive and a rash person.

- Students should practise using the words straight away – for example, they could finish off a sentence that includes the word: "The most impulsive thing I have ever done is …" Perhaps they could take part in a class discussion about Romeo's impulsive actions in the play.

- Students should have multiple exposures to new words, otherwise they are unlikely to learn them securely – for example, they might be encouraged to use impulsive in subsequent discussions and essay writing.

Beck et al. provide a useful three-tier taxonomy to help you choose words for closer inspection. Tier 1 words are basic words that young people will pick up through ordinary conversation: book, clock, run and table, for instance. Tier 2 words are unlikely to be encountered regularly in ordinary speech but can be found in academic texts, broadsheet newspapers or challenging literary fiction. Examples include coincidence, absurd and industrious. Last of all, tier 3 words tend to be limited to specific subject disciplines – examples from English include anaphora, protagonist and tragedy.

A sensible approach in English lessons is to concentrate on subject-specific tier 3 words and high-frequency tier 2 words. The tier 2 words might include generic words to describe a character's behaviour and feelings (imperturbable, despairing, naive) or verbs to use in analytical writing (amplifies, reinforces, downplays).

Ultimately, if our students are to develop their academic vocabularies, our classrooms must become places where words are constantly explored, discussed and experimented with. Students must develop their word awareness and curiosity. So how can we do this?

♦ Create a vocabulary list for each new unit of work. A unit on *An Inspector Calls* might include terms to describe the characters, like 'aristocratic', 'haughty' and 'omniscient', and literary terms like 'morality play', 'monologue', 'dialogue' and 'denouement'. Ensure that you teach the words as and when they are pertinent to the part of the text you are teaching, and use the list to devise spelling tests and quizzes. Be flexible too. Part of the fun is adapting the list as you go.

♦ Teach two or three new vocabulary words a lesson. Choose words integral to the content of the lesson, and expect students to continue using these words in subsequent lessons. Again, find ways to keep the words 'live' through quizzes, games and discussion. Praise those who make the conscious effort to use them.

♦ Model your love of words by being prepared to discuss new vocabulary when it crops up. Do not be afraid to go off-piste for a bit. Some words need careful teacher explanation; others can be left for the students to tease out the meaning themselves. Study the morphology of words by breaking them into prefixes, suffixes and roots. Not only does this help students to understand the building blocks of language, but it also makes the word more memorable. Be aware that this is not always possible. Consider the difference between 'other-worldliness' which can be broken up and figured out, and 'melancholy' which requires direct teaching.

♦ Insist your students use precise vocabulary in class discussions. This simple but powerful habit is exemplified in the dialogue below:

Teacher: So how does Juliet feel at this point?

Student: She feels like she wants to kill herself.

Teacher: Can you find a more suitable word for that?

Student: She feels suicidal.

♦ Find the story behind the word by examining its etymology. We understand the word 'hypocrite' more precisely when we discover that it originates from the Ancient Greek for 'actor' – one who constantly changes roles. In truth, we are far more likely to remember a word's meaning when it comes complete with a postage-stamp sized biography.

♦ 'Ban' overused words and phrases. On my list are 'scared', 'nice', 'upset' and 'it makes the reader want to read on'. Encourage students to look for more subtle alternatives. Or teach these directly.

♦ Be fun and playful with language and model your own curiosity for words. Greet your boisterous Year 9s with: "Ladies and gents, you're all rather exuberant today!" Praise John with: "Wow, John, you're completely irrepressible this afternoon!" I once dedicated ten minutes of a Year 9 lesson to explaining the expression 'a damp squib'. Many in the class subsequently took up my challenge to drop the phrase as nonchalantly as they could into a conversation with their parents that evening!

In summary, invest time in developing your students' vocabulary. Ludwig Wittgenstein had it right: "The limits of my language mean the limits of my world."

Reflective Questions

♦ Do you choose texts that immerse students in new and challenging vocabulary, linguistic structures, concepts and contexts?

♦ Do you direct students towards the background knowledge and vocabulary they need to understand and analyse challenging literature?

♦ Are your students developing the habit of grappling with difficult texts?

Chapter 2
Explaining and Questioning Reading

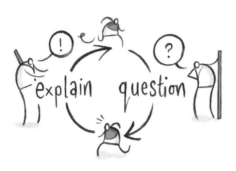

She bridled a little

Your class are reading chapter 2 of John Steinbeck's Of Mice and Men *when they come to this sentence: "Lennie's eyes moved down over her body, and though she didn't seem to be looking at Lennie she bridled a little."*

"What can we infer about Curley's wife's behaviour here?" you ask.

Silence.

You scan the room, while your students do their best not to catch your eye. You ask Aaron for his opinion.

"I don't know."

"How about the way she 'bridled a little' after Lennie stares at her? What do you think?"

Silence again.

"Okay, let me explain. To 'bridle' means to show your anger or resentment by throwing up your head and drawing in your chin." (You accompany your explanation with a thespian flick of your head.)

Slowly, a few tentative hands are raised. You're back in business.

The above is a common scenario. On this occasion, lack of comprehension, rather than apathy or laziness, caused the awkwardness. The guilty culprit was 'bridled'. Once this verb had been understood, the students were able to answer the question.

This is why teacher explanation plays a vital role in improving reading. It is only possible to make a good inference about a passage when you have a good grasp of its literal meaning. As with the Curley's wife example, your classes will sometimes need you to tell them the answer.

There is a fear that 'telling' can restrict creativity and originality. However, if we want to encourage critical and divergent thinking, then we must provide our students with the tools they need to do this. If we don't, then young people must resort to plucking ideas out of the ether, the educational equivalent of alchemy. When implemented carefully, explicit teaching can have a wonderful effect in the English classroom. It can induct students in the discipline of the subject and spark genuine insight.

Nevertheless, it requires subtlety. Good readers process meaning for themselves, which is why your classes must also be given the space to grapple with a tough text on their own, even if they misinterpret the text along the way. We cannot teach a child to read by always telling them what a text means. Yet it is equally unhelpful to expect a child to fathom out all the meaning from a difficult text for themselves. Our aim, therefore, is to strike a balance between dependence and independence.

At times we must take control; at other times cede control. We should always be prepared to adjust our lessons, but we should not forget that our aim is to help our class to read challenging texts on their own.

Before planning a lesson on reading it is important to take heed of the differences between strong and weak readers. Reading experts tend to agree that those who are skilled at automatic inferencing have the following factors in common:

- A competent working memory.
- An active desire to make sense of the text.
- Motivation to fill in their knowledge gaps.
- The ability to monitor comprehension and repair inconsistencies.
- The same cultural background as that assumed by the text.
- A rich vocabulary.
- A wide background knowledge.

On the other hand, less able readers are less aware:

♦ That a text should make sense.

♦ That they should be monitoring their understanding for inconsistencies.

♦ Of the kind of strategies to adopt when embarking on reading a text.

♦ Of which strategies to use when an inconsistency occurs.

♦ Of the need to draw inferences at all.

♦ Of the kind of information that is relevant to the drawing of inferences.

We should always shape our explanations and questions around these findings and insights when working with students across the range of reading abilities.

1. Break It Up

How can I organise the reading of difficult texts so that my classes do not become overwhelmed?

Research shows that effective teachers present new material in small steps with student practice after each stage.[1] This reduces cognitive load – the amount of mental effort being employed in the working memory – and means that students are more likely to understand and retain the content they have read. The more tricky and dense the text, the more chunks it probably should be broken into.

---

1 See Barak Rosenshine, Principles of Instruction: Research-Based Strategies That All Teachers Should Know, *American Educator* (spring 2012): 12–19. Available at: https://www.aft.org/sites/default/files/periodicals/Rosenshine.pdf.

A challenging poem or Shakespearean soliloquy, for instance, might need a verse-by-verse or line-by-line breakdown – although you should always read the text in full first so that it is experienced as the complete work of art it was created to be. On the other hand, a Key Stage 3 young adult novel will require far fewer breaks. Less challenging texts like these should be used to build your students' reading stamina and their ability to cope with extended spells of unbroken concentration.

Strategies for breaking up texts include:

- **Double readings.** Take a few lessons to read the full text quickly for basic comprehension. Then dip into sections (or the whole text if you have time) again to provoke deeper analysis and insight. The tricky passages and labyrinthine plot of Robert Louis Stevenson's the *Strange Case of Dr Jekyll and Mr Hyde*, for example, can be tackled on a first reading. On a second reading, Stevenson's themes, characterisation and use of symbolism can be given closer scrutiny. After all, until you realise that Jekyll and Hyde are one person you cannot unpick Stevenson's ideas about the duality of man! Always remember that many students – and well-educated adults – find it very hard to make sophisticated interpretations and linkages on a first reading.

- **Forward and back.** A similar approach is to divide your schemes of work into paired lessons. The first lesson might involve reading a chapter, a scene or a poem for understanding. In the second, you might extend upon and deepen this understanding.

- **Discuss before writing.** After reading a complicated passage of text you can choose whether to switch directly to independent work or begin with a teacher-led class discussion. The latter allows you to scaffold and support comprehension before the independent work.

2. Prime Them

How can I prepare my students to make good inferences?

Preparation is everything. The climber packs his rope, the gardener tills the soil and readers of challenging texts need similar priming. In other words, they need some prior knowledge to apply to what they are to read so that they can begin to construct meaning and make sound inferences for themselves. Priming has a number of aims: to spark curiosity, to provide something to 'stick' new learning to and to provide a rough outline – a nascent mental representation – of what is to come.

For example, how might you prime a class for their first reading of the prologue to *Romeo and Juliet*? Several strategies could be employed, alone or in combination:

♦ **Three quotations.** Before reading the entire prologue, introduce three quotations that offer a gateway into the play – perhaps 'ancient-grudge', 'star-cross'd lovers' and 'death-mark'd love'. Ensure that the students understand the literal meanings and start to connect them together.

♦ **Themes first.** Choose a theme or two – love and fate, for instance. Explore these as a class. What do they mean? What is their importance to the modern world? How do they relate to each other?

♦ **Contextual cues.** Teach the historical context first. An introduction to the role of parents, children and women in the Elizabethan era will help your class to understand why Romeo and Juliet's love affair was so hazardous.

♦ **Related non-fiction.** The pairing of fiction and non-fiction texts is highly recommended by Doug Lemov, Colleen Driggs and Erica Woolway in *Reading Reconsidered*. Your class could read a non-fiction text before you introduce them to the prologue – perhaps a description of courtly conventions in Elizabethan times or even a modern news story of thwarted love, if you can source an appropriate one.

♦ **Descriptive adjectives.** Provide a list of abstract nouns, or adjectives that describe feelings and atmospheres. For the prologue, you could choose sorrow, violence, hope, tragedy and regret. Students should use these to annotate the text and then should justify their annotations.

♦ **A question.** Do the groundwork by getting your class to think first. What information might a playwright include in a prologue? What might a playwright choose not to include? Why tell an audience how the play will unfold before it has even started?

There are plenty of other imaginative priming methods you could try. They are most useful with difficult texts such as poetry, Shakespeare and dense sections of nineteenth century novels. As you delve further into the text, confidence and comprehension will begin to improve, and at this point you can begin to allow students more autonomy by removing these support mechanisms.

3. Question After

How can I help my students to make interesting comments about texts?

Most English teachers ask a series of quick, intense questions after they have read a passage of text. There are two key components to this: questioning for understanding (surface questions) and questioning for analysis (deep questions). To plan a question sequence you need to decide on the endpoint you want your students to reach. This might range from an interpretation of a character's motives to an analysis of a literary technique.

Let's imagine your class have just read the following passage from Arthur Conan Doyle's 'The Adventure of the Speckled Band', in which the villain, the irascible Dr Roylott, barges into Sherlock Holmes' rooms.

The ejaculation had been drawn from my companion by the fact that our door had been suddenly dashed open, and that a huge man had framed himself in the aperture. His costume was a peculiar mixture of the professional and of the agricultural, having a black top-hat, a long frock-coat, and a pair of high gaiters, with a hunting-crop swinging in his hand. So tall was he that his hat actually brushed the cross bar of the doorway, and his breadth seemed to span it across from side to side.

Your aim is for your students to describe how Conan Doyle has created a menacing, threatening character in Dr Roylott, almost to the point of caricature. In the following sequence, you employ four intertwined questioning techniques:

1   Questions for understanding (QU)

2   Questions for analysis (QA)

3   Probing questions (PQ)

4   Mini-explanations (ME)

You anticipate more than a few raised eyebrows at the word 'ejaculation' so you aim to nip this in the bud:

You: In this section we have met Dr Roylott for the first time. In the first sentence, the word 'ejaculation' means that somebody has cried out in surprise. (ME) *Who cries out ... Jess?* (QU)

Jess: It's Holmes.

You: Yes, and why has he cried out? (QU)

Jess: Because Roylott has come in the door.

You: Conan Doyle uses the verb 'dashed' to describe the way it opens. (ME) *Why do you think he used this word rather than, say, 'pushed'?* (QA)

Jess: It has opened quickly.

You: What impression does this give you about Roylott? (QA/ PQ)

Jess: Maybe he is angry and threatening and out to get Holmes.

You: Good. Now, everybody, could you please scan through the paragraph and find another word or phrase that also makes him seem threatening and imposing. Put your finger on the quotation when you have found one. You have thirty seconds. Go. (QU)

Your class read out a list: 'huge man', 'framed himself in the aperture', 'hunting-crop swinging in his hand', 'hat actually brushed the cross bar of the doorway' and 'his breadth seemed to span it'. Before moving on, you explain quickly what a hunting-crop is. (ME)

You: Which of these is the most threatening image? (pause) *James, what do you think?* (QA)

James: I think it's the hunting-crop image.

You: Why's that then? (PQ)

James: Well, it is like he has a weapon that he is about to strike someone with.

You: Good. What are the connotations of this image? (QA) (Only use this question if your class are habitualised to look for connotations.)

James: Well, it makes us think of predators and their prey, as if Roylott is a predator who is hunting down Holmes.

You: Excellent analysis. Now, which image do you think is the most exaggerated one – as if it comes from a cartoon … Tom? (QU)

Tom: I think it's the one about him spanning the breadth of the doorway. I mean, no one is really that wide, are they?

You: Interesting. Now, this is a hard question. Why would Conan Doyle want to make Roylott seem like such an obvious criminal? Doesn't it give the game away? (QA)

Abbie: Well, I think it's a red herring. He wants us to think that Roylott is the villain when really he's not. He's manipulating the reader.

You: Ooh, that's interesting. Put your hand up if you agree with Abbie. Sam, your hand is down – what's your view? (PQ)

Sam: Well, perhaps it's a double bluff. He wants to make Dr Roylott such an obvious villain that we think he's a red herring, when really it's him who killed Miss Stoner. He's the villain …

This is an example of interactive whole-class questioning – you might include short paired discussions too. The golden rule is to shift between closed questions (questions for understanding) and open questions (questions for analysis). Sequences that switch the focus back and forth between understanding and analysis help to model the relationship between the literal meaning of a text and its wider implications. The adept English teacher knows just the right time to make these transitions.

Finally, never be afraid to abandon the questioning sequence. However probing and adroit your questions are, the students will not always play ball. Sometimes you will need to cut your losses and take over yourself. At other times, the discussion will take you in unexpected directions along fruitful and untrodden paths. There's no need to feel guilty if your students do not cotton on to Conan Doyle's double bluff immediately. By explaining it, you will hand them a thinking tool to apply to the next detective story they read.

4. Make It Concrete

How can I bring difficult contexts and concepts to life?

Cognitive science has revealed that we take on board new information by fastening it to the things we already know.[2] Literature, however, presents young people with people, places, emotions and experiences beyond the confines of their own lives. They are dropped into the mindscapes of saints and tyrants and into the courts and marketplaces of pre-Renaissance Italy and Victorian London. For many, these fictional recreations lay on a feast for the imagination, yet for others, they can feel alien and obscure – far removed from life in twenty-first century Britain. As English teachers, our role is to ensure that these concepts and contexts become coherent and conceivable.

There are three approaches to help you achieve this: images, graphs/diagrams and drama.

---

2   Deans for Impact, *The Science of Learning* (Austin, TX: Deans for Impact, 2015). Available at: http://deansforimpact.org/pdfs/The_Science_of_Learning.pdf.

1. Through images

Cognitive science suggests that the simultaneous presentation of visual and verbal material has been shown to improve learning – the dual-coding theory. An image can encapsulate a concept with wonderful concision. When my low-achieving Year 10 class were struggling to grasp the concept of dramatic irony, a quick Google search led me to the famous *Jaws* film poster (a monstrous shark rising from the deep under a blissfully unaware swimmer). I shared it with the group and, hey presto, dramatic irony finally clicked.

Blogger and English teacher Phil Stock, an enthusiastic advocate of the use of images to enhance learning, has shared the following evidence-informed advice on how to use them effectively:[3]

♦ Pair words and images.

♦ Choose images to aid learning, not to entertain.

♦ Keep images near the text.

♦ Choose simple, not complicated, images.

♦ Strip out the text, especially if the image is self-explanatory.

♦ Get students drawing (great for representing complex concepts).

♦ Use visual–spatial representations to show connections between ideas.

And never forget the important supporting role that films and documentaries can play when they are used judiciously alongside the original text.

---

3 Phil Stock, 'Without Contraries There Is No Progression': Or 7 Principles for Pairing Words with Images, *Must Do Better …* (12 June 2016). Available at: https://joeybagstock.wordpress.com/2016/06/12/without-contraries-there-is-no-progression-or-7-principles-for-pairing-words-with-images/.

2. Through graphs and diagrams

Simple graphs and diagrams can help students to get a handle on the underlying patterns of a text. Plot, character and theme development all benefit from simple line graphs. The rising and falling tension of a Shakespearean tragedy can be brilliantly represented in this way: from the exposition, to the inciting force, to the hamartia, to the high point of the crisis, and then downwards to the tragic force, to the final moment of suspense and, finally, to the glimpse of restored order – which gives your graph a desultory flick in the tail.

Other forms of visual–spatial representation are also beneficial. Venn diagrams are excellent for considering comparisons within and between texts. Pie charts help with comparing the levels of reader sympathy for characters. Mind-maps are valuable for forging connections between themes, characters and the writer's intentions. Maps and plans can help students to visualise settings. Finally, graphs and diagrams provide wonderful catalysts for discussion. Don't just create them, discuss them too.

3. Through drama

Drama is an English teacher's Marmite – you either love it or hate it. Whatever your personal preference, when drama is conducted well it can illuminate the emotional content of a text and lift the mood and attention of the class. English teacher Sue Wolstenholme was an expert at designing very short (under ten minute) dramatic reconstructions. These would be used before or after reading a pivotal episode in a text. Her class might recreate an event from a novel – such as the fight between Curley and Lennie in chapter 3 of *Of Mice and Men* – or they might invent situations attached to a historical story – such as an interview with a Light Brigade soldier just before the infamous suicidal charge.

This example comes from Sue's teaching of *Macbeth*. In Act 5, Scene 5, Macbeth hears the tragic news about his wife: "The queen, my lord, is dead." Before launching into the famous monologue that follows, Sue would ask a confident student to come to the front to play Macbeth. The class would then direct the student, guided all the time by Sue's incisive questioning:

- Where is Macbeth standing?
- Will he be facing the window, scanning the horizon for the oncoming English army, or will he be looking elsewhere?
- Will he stop what he is doing?
- Will he slow down?
- What will he do with his hands?
- What will be going on in his mind?
- Has he felt like this before?
- Have his feelings changed from earlier in the play?
- When he responds, what will his tone of voice and body language be like?
- How will he deliver his next line – "She should have died hereafter"?

The objective of Sue's approach was to shed light on a moment in the play and to develop it in great detail, not to act out the whole scene. Her aim was to create a visual and emotional context for the reading that would follow – another example of priming. As long as they are used to support understanding (rather than to entertain the class), drama strategies like Sue's can be extremely effective.

5. Go Intertextual

How can I help my students to transfer their knowledge from text to text?

If we learn in the context of what we already know, then an intertextual approach to reading can deliver plenty of riches. This involves the search for the similarities, differences and connections between texts – explicit and implicit – as well as a consideration of how texts allude to and find inspiration in each other. It is easy to fall into the trap of approaching each new text as a single, atomised unit, divorced from literary tradition.

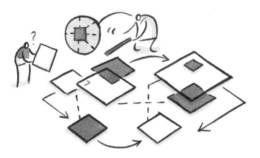

By drawing attention to the interconnectedness of texts, we help our students to make the associative links that are so important to embedding new learning. Literary studies is an academic discipline in its own right and it is underpinned by a number of essential concepts, tropes and techniques. Think of narrative structure, characterisation, symbolism and imagery. All writers employ these but in very different ways. Each new text adds to your students' growing knowledge about these common concepts so that they can tackle the next text they read with greater autonomy, authority and confidence.

There are three obvious ways to promote understanding of intertextuality: explanations, questions and tasks.

1. Intertextual explanations

When explaining new ideas and concepts, refer to texts you have already read. Not only does this gift-wrap for your class some handy revision, but it also provides a meaningful shared context – a bottomless well that keeps on giving. For example, you might teach the term 'protagonist' by referring to the lead characters in texts they have already read, or you might introduce the term 'internal conflict' by comparing two characters from separate texts:

Stanhope is suffering from an internal conflict. Does he submit and go home a coward, or does he fight on to the bitter end? This reminds us of George from Of Mice and Men who had his own internal conflict. Should he go through life independently, leaving Lennie to the cruel hands of fate and society, or should he protect his only friend and companion?

Similarly, encourage your students to explain their understanding of new texts by asking them to make comparisons with previous texts.

2. Intertextual questions

Drop intertextual questions into lessons whenever possible. Your students should be expected to answer them verbally or in writing. They can provoke considered, fine-grained discrimination:

Mr Birling and Scrooge are both middle class businessmen. What are the main differences in how they are presented by Priestley and Dickens?

Who provokes the most audience/reader sympathy: Eva Smith or Tiny Tim?

Or, to really challenge your students, you could try:

Who would be the better prime minister: William Shakespeare, J. B. Priestley or Charles Dickens? Use evidence from their texts to support your viewpoint.

3. Intertextual tasks

Venn diagrams are, again, an excellent choice for comparing characterisation and authorial viewpoint. Lessons that focus on how concepts, themes and literary techniques work across texts, rather than within texts, can work brilliantly. A lesson on Biblical allusion could span three texts: *Romeo and Juliet, An Inspector Calls* and the *Strange Case of Dr Jekyll and Mr Hyde*. A lesson on pathetic fallacy could span a whole anthology of poetry.

Reflective Questions

♦ Do you teach sophisticated interpretations of texts directly?

♦ Do you reduce cognitive load by priming students with background knowledge and 'broken-up' reading?

♦ Do you guide your students towards successful reading habits by alternating questions for understanding and questions for analysis?

- ♦ Are your students encouraged to find connections between texts so that they are immersed in the academic discipline of English?

Chapter 3

Modelling Reading

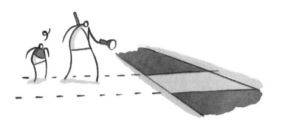

Futility

Isabelle's class have been studying First World War poetry. So far, they have read two Wilfred Owen poems, 'Dulce et Decorum est' and 'Anthem for Doomed Youth'. Isabelle's exercise book is crammed full of detailed notes and she has a firm grasp of both poems.

Now Isabelle's teacher would like her class to read a third Owen poem, 'Futility' – this time with less support. She hands out the poem and gives the class ten minutes to read and annotate independently. Helpfully, she provides a glossary covering the more challenging words and phrases.

Isabelle reads the poem once and stops. She puts her head on the desk where it remains for the next nine minutes.

Reading a hard poem independently requires a set of tactics. For experienced poetry readers like you and me, these tactics are probably already in place. They have been honed over time. We might read the poem through two or three times until we get the gist. We might single out phrases that seem unusual or of greater importance – "Woke once the limbs of a cold star", for instance. We might notice literary devices at play, such as the personification of the sun in Owen's poem. We might strive to put our finger on the overall message of the poem. However we do it, the process is invisible and automatic. We hardly need to think about it.

Isabelle, however, is a relative novice. She needs to be shown how to pick apart a poem. Perhaps her teacher could have demonstrated some useful strategies with an earlier poem. A valuable approach is to narrate your thoughts out loud: "Now, I don't quite get this line, so I'm going to start the verse again. Perhaps it relies on an earlier clause ..." Even more usefully, her teacher might have introduced a simple stepped procedure for the class to follow, or perhaps the class and teacher could have created one together:

1   Read the poem once.

2   Read it again.

3   Circle three phrases you find interesting. Annotate them.

4   Find three poetic devices. Write down the effect they create.

5   Write a sentence explaining what you think the main message of the poem is.

The goal of modelling reading, therefore, is to shine a light on implicit, invisible metacognitive processes so that they feel simple and achievable.[1] A support structure like this would allow Isabelle to self-regulate her close reading.

In fact, there are plenty of sophisticated reading skills that should be modelled. These include language analysis, the identification of alternative interpretations, the evaluation of reader responses and how to respond critically to a text. However, do not forget to model foundational skills too; skimming and scanning, finding quotations and even how to

---

1   For strong evidence on the impact of metacognition see: https://educationendowmentfoundation.org.uk/resources/teaching-learning-toolkit/meta-cognition-and-self-regulation.

keep your place during whole-class shared reading all benefit from explicit modelling.

As well as modelling reading skills and strategies, English teachers should also model reading dispositions. The best teachers model curiosity and deep contemplation. They model an openness to alternative viewpoints and an appetite and enthusiasm for linguistic ingenuity. They also model the tentative, exploratory language of literary criticism, even with their least proficient students.

In this chapter, therefore, we will cover the four corner-stones of the modelling of reading: explode it, whittle it down, suggest it and read it out loud.

1. Explode It

How do I model the thinking processes of a critical and analytical reader?

When asked to analyse a passage of text, good readers cover it with marginalia. They home in on the slippery bits and draw boxes and circles around crucial words. They search for patterns and link sections of text with arrows. They cram the empty spaces with questions and short, scribbled notes. They dig deep down into a text, discovering and crys-tallising meaning. This is the process of annotation.

Modelling the annotation process with your classes allows you to demonstrate the practicalities of 'marking up' a text. It also provides a visual guide to your thought processes as a reader. Yet annotation is much more than simply writing notes on a projected text. It is a process that needs to be taught in a carefully staged way, allowing ample time for practice.

To start with, give students short quotations to annotate, rather than dense chunks of text. This allows them to concentrate on the process itself. Some English teachers call this 'quote explosion'. It is incredibly effective and the students tend to make more detailed notes than they do when they have to find the quotations and evidence for themselves.

Let's say you have shown your class these lines spoken by Lady Macbeth:

Come, you spirits

That tend on mortal thoughts, unsex me here,

And fill me from the crown to the toe top-full

Of direst cruelty!

Before annotating, define with the class what they should be looking for. You might choose a close focus such as, "Annotate the ways in which these lines show Lady Macbeth's innermost desires", or you might leave it open. Either way, your students need a clear, tick-list procedure to work through.

Perhaps you could ask them to:

♦ Circle any words/phrases that seem important or interesting (even if you are not sure why).

♦ Label any literary devices that you notice.

♦ Choose at least two words or phrases to 'zoom in' on (if you have a close focus, these will provide the answer).

♦ Make a link to the play's historical context.

♦ Write down one question.

Here is a worked example:

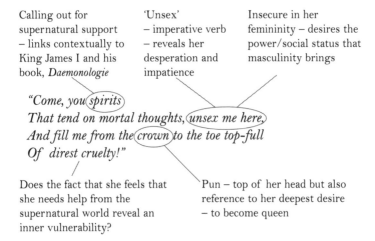

Calling out for supernatural support – links contextually to King James I and his book, *Daemonologie*

'Unsex' – imperative verb – reveals her desperation and impatience

Insecure in her femininity – desires the power/social status that masculinity brings

"Come, you spirits
That tend on mortal thoughts, unsex me here,
And fill me from the crown to the toe top-full
Of direst cruelty!"

Does the fact that she feels that she needs help from the supernatural world reveal an inner vulnerability?

Pun – top of her head but also reference to her deepest desire – to become queen

At first, model this for the class, using the tick-list to guide your thoughts. After this, reveal a second quotation and annotate it with the help of the class. Then they can annotate a third quotation in pairs. Finally, they should attempt one on their own.

Once the students are confident with annotating pre-extracted quotations, move on to complete passages. Again, model the process with a section of text – perhaps a single paragraph to start with – and, again, share a clear focus for the annotation. This time, talk through the process of selection, explaining why some phrases offer richer pickings than others. Provide a procedural tick-list, and remove support slowly and carefully until the students are working independently.

There are countless other ways to annotate a text. A very effective strategy is to model critical reading by annotating the omissions, inconsistencies, assumptions and biases of a text with questions:

♦ Yes, but what about …?

♦ Is this always the case?

♦ Has the writer ignored …?

♦ Doesn't this contradict …?

♦ How strong is the evidence?

♦ What has the writer failed to mention?

The key point is that whichever form of annotation you choose to teach, remember to model the procedure first.

2. Whittle It Down

How do I help my students to discriminate between good and bad ideas?

I think the bird in the poem that is flying up in the sky symbolises his soul going up to heaven. He will now be in peace forever.

John, 13

Has a student of yours ever fallen back on a superficial cliché like John's? I bet they have.

Once a student begins to recognise that literature is rich with implicit symbolic meaning, he is on his way to becoming a sophisticated reader. However, his initial attempts at interpretation may seem shallow or fail to hit the mark – as with John's heavenly bird. This is why our students must learn that not all readings are equal and that some are more precise than others. They must also learn that the ability to weigh up alternative interpretations – even those that challenge our own – is one of the hallmarks of a mature reader.

How can we model this kind of discrimination? Sarah Donarski, an English teacher at Wellington College, has developed a powerfully simple strategy. Her walls are not festooned in decorative displays. Instead, Sarah has permanent wraparound whiteboards. When Sarah needs to hear her class's thoughts, she asks her students to write on the walls. Once complete, Sarah has a visual representation of the range and depth of the students' ideas.

The valuable bit comes next. The class collaborate to separate the strong ideas from the flimsy, the insightful from the superficial. This process of discrimination is so often buried away in a student's mind. In Sarah's room, however, it is writ large. Quite literally.

Of course, not all of us have the luxury of wall-to-wall whiteboards. Despite this, there are plenty of ways that you can emulate Sarah's strategy in your classroom. Since speaking with Sarah, I have modified my responses to student answers after an open question. Instead of commenting on their responses immediately – once my go-to approach – I now list their verbal answers on the board without comment. Then, together, we will choose the most perceptive and insightful to run with.

The ultimate aim of this whittling down approach is that students learn that their first idea is not always the best. Over time, they should begin to develop a feeling – a sixth sense – for what makes a strong literary interpretation.

3. Suggest It

How do I encourage my students to think, speak and write like literary critics?

Literary study is an unusual discipline that presents unique challenges for our students. Unlike mathematics and science, English is less about the quest for objective truth. Once reading basics – decoding, comprehension and fluency – are in place, a student is instead shunted into the realm of interpretation, inference and insight. This can be a confusing place. It's easy to see why many prefer the security of the two-dimensional logic of right and wrong.

Be this as it may, we need our students to think, speak and write in an academic style. This kind of critical discourse is tentative and suggestive. It delights in ambiguity. It seeks out paradox and rejects absolutes in favour of uncertainty.

Some simple strategies can help to embed this. First, we should model the language of literary discourse in our speech and writing whenever possible. Second, we should make this salient. Third, we should take every opportunity to encourage it in our students' speech and writing.

The following phrases are useful for this kind of 'hedging':

♦ Perhaps this …

♦ The writer might have/may have/could have …

♦ This appears to …

♦ The writer tends to …

♦ It is possible that …

♦ This seems …

♦ The reader is caught between …

♦ This suggests/implies …

- Some might argue that …; however, others might believe that …

- Notice the way that …

- It is almost as if …

- Even though the character usually displays the qualities of decency and compassion …

- The writer hints that …

Use these purposefully in your talk, in your written modelling (see Chapter 7) and in the sentence starters you share. Pin them up in a visible place. Glue them into your students' books. Over time, expect your students to use them in their speech and writing, and make a point of praising them when they do. Of course, there are also times for more confident assertions: the verbs 'shows', 'indicates' and 'reveals' are useful in these situations. However, the hideous phrases 'this proves that' and 'I know this because …' should be actively discouraged!

The twin concepts of connotation and association should also be prioritised. Students should come to understand that words evoke ideas and feelings in addition to their literal or primary meaning. Start introducing this concept as soon as you can – from Year 7 if you are a secondary teacher – and pay special attention to the notion that the same word can have both positive and negative connotations and associations.

Remember, too, the central role of questioning. Asking a question conveys a subliminal message. I am not the arbiter of all knowledge. Like you, I am still searching for meaning.

This comes with a qualification. English teachers should never be afraid to teach. We should always be prepared to be the sage on the stage as well as the guide on the side. Many facts, critical perspectives and interpretations will be new to students and beyond the scope of their current knowledge.

The best approach is to explain these clearly and carefully as you will not be able to elicit them if students don't have the foundations to draw from.

Does this contradict the earlier point about the subjectivity of English? No. John Wolstenholme talks about the difference between telling a student what to think ('This means ...') and making a suggestion about what they could think ('This might mean ...'). The first is rigid and inflexible: it teaches a new idea as an incontrovertible fact rather than as a cautious assertion. The second is much more helpful. Not only does it hand your class a ready-made idea to think about, but it once again models the tentative and exploratory discourse of literary criticism.

Even your posture has a role to play. You can model contemplative listening by holding your chin, nodding slowly and furrowing your brow, and if, like me, you wear spectacles, you could even accompany this with a quizzically professorial stare over your frames!

4. Read It Out Loud

How do I best model my love of the subject?

Reading out loud is one of the forgotten arts of English teaching. It can be magical. The best reading can entice a child into a shared imaginative space where walls, chairs, desks – and even teachers – seem to diminish and slip away. On the flip side, however, monotonous and tedious reading can become a barrier to understanding and enjoyment.

Sue Wolstenholme was an expert at reading out loud. (I can personally testify just how utterly captivating her reading could be and the hypnotic effect it would have on students.) Nevertheless, Sue emphasises that good reading out loud is no God-given talent; it is a skill that any teacher can learn with practice and dedication.

Sue suggests that we should always read as if we ourselves are experiencing the text for the first time. However, she stresses that reading out loud is an act and, like all theatre, should be rehearsed beforehand. There is much to prepare: the voices of each character; the episodes to be read with pace; the moments to hold the class in a pause; the questions to ask; the times to stop and look up. Sue also suggests that we should plan where in the classroom we will read from, when we will move and when we will stand still.

Sue credits much of her success as a teacher to the quality of her reading. The intensity of the experience would spur many children to want to read more books by the same author. It would help students to acknowledge that reading can bring pleasure and excitement. It would help them to pick up new phrases and words without being aware of it. It would help them to hear the rhythms of sentences and phraseology which would support them when they were reading independently.

Similarly, Doug Lemov, Colleen Driggs and Erica Woolway point to how hearing a teacher read develops synaptic control. This is "the capacity to use forms of grammar to build sentences and construct ideas with flexibility and fluidity".[2] Reading aloud also helps us to capture the prosody of language – the stresses and intonations – and it plays an

---

2   Lemov et al., *Reading Reconsidered*, p. 240.

essential role in modelling how to read with fluency.[3] Therefore, hearing an adult read aloud from a text that is currently beyond your reading capability – in terms of vocabulary and content – is a very powerful learning experience.

Here are five top tips to improve your reading out loud:

1   Record or video your reading and play it back to gauge its expressiveness and musicality.

2   Listen to high-quality spoken word recordings of texts you are about to teach (you can find many on YouTube). Consider how the oration is modified by switches in pace and tone, when pauses are used, how dialogue is incorporated and how emphasis is placed on certain words.

3   Try to 'live' the story as you read. Over time, you will find that you develop the curious ability to read out loud and think about something else at the same time. Try to fight this as it can spoil the authenticity of your performance.

4   Share the reading of less complex texts with your students. Many teachers start a shared reading session to set the tone and then pass responsibility over to the students.

5   If you find reading with expression a struggle, try to place extra emphasis on at least one word in every sentence, especially those that emphasise some kind of contrast. For instance: "It is a truth universally acknowledged, that a single *man* in possession of a good fortune, must be in want of a *wife*."

In sum, there is no better way of modelling your love and passion for English than through the way you read out loud.

---

3   See Daniel T. Willingham, *Raising Kids Who Read: What Parents and Teachers Can Do* (San Francisco, CA: Jossey-Bass, 2015), p. 137.

Reflective Questions

♦ Do you repeatedly model a full range of reading strategies so that the implicit habits of proficient readers become explicit?

♦ Do you direct students towards the steps they need in order to perform complex reading procedures?

♦ Are your students immersed in the suggestive and tentative language of literary critical discourse?

♦ Do you pay special attention to your reading aloud so that your students become immersed in the rhythms and patterns of language?

Chapter 4

Practising Reading

Impenetrable terrain?

Mr Shoehorn hands his Year 11 class a practice reading exam question, an article written about a remote region of eastern Russia, the Kamchatka Peninsula. The task is as follows:

Using your own words, explain what the writer means by the words in italics in the following phrase: 'the *terrain* is so *impenetrable*'.

Two marks are available, one for each correctly explained word.

Answers that read, 'the ground/country is so impassable' (or similar) are credited with two marks.

Mr Shoehorn is shocked. Out of a class of twenty-five 15–16-year-olds, only one achieves both marks. Most get neither. Although the majority of class members are comfortable with the meaning of penetrate, very few understand the term terrain.

Young people who fail to comprehend the phrase 'the terrain is so impenetrable' are young people who have not spent enough of their lives reading challenging texts. Daniel Rigney has written about the difference between the 'word rich' and the 'word poor'. He has termed it the 'Matthew effect'.[1] As the rich get richer, the poor get poorer. This is why practice is the most crucial element to reading and it explains why so many in Mr Shoehorn's lesson were left confused. By Year 11, the yawning reading chasm was too wide to be filled.

Reading will always be harder for some children than it is for others. Twin studies are revealing more and more about the complex interplay between genes and environment, and how these combine to influence cognitive ability and educational achievement. Recent studies suggest that approximately 60–80% of the differences in reading ability between individuals might be attributed to heritable factors.[2]

Put bluntly, individual differences in reading ability are inevitable. However, this does not explain why Mr Shoehorn's students, whose attainment levels were broadly average, could not comprehend the sentence. K. Anders Ericsson, the world-renowned expert on the benefits of practice, argues that people have a tendency to practise to a certain point and then stop in the belief that they cannot go any further. Ericsson argues that with better, more purposeful practice, there are few impediments that most people could not conquer.[3] What Mr Shoehorn's students needed, therefore, was more frequent and better quality reading practice in the years leading up to Year 11.

Practice is the active part of learning. It requires effort, determination, resilience and a whole host of non-cognitive

---

1   Daniel Rigney, *The Matthew Effect: How Advantage Begets Further Advantage* (New York and Chichester: Columbia University Press, 2010).

2   Kathryn Asbury and Robert Plomin, *G is for Genes: The Impact of Genetics on Education and Achievement* (Chichester: John Wiley, 2013), p. 24.

3   K. Anders Ericsson and Robert Pool, *Peak: Secrets from the New Science of Expertise* (New York: Houghton Mifflin, 2016).

skills. Those who find pleasure and joy in reading find it far easier to practise.

In this chapter, we will examine three types of practice that are essential for academic success: independent reading practice, processing practice and retrieval practice.

1. Read Alone

How do I support my students to read independently?

Academic research and teacher experience all point to one thing: children who read for pleasure are more likely to be academically successful than those who do not.[4] It is imperative, therefore, that we support our students to become competent and independent readers. This is not as easy as it sounds. The following three methods should be used together over a sustained period of time.

1. Unassisted reading

DEAR (Drop Everything And Read) is usually a whole-school literacy initiative. All students bring a book and sit silently and read on a daily or weekly basis. In many schools, teachers allow students to choose their own books. Other schools use systems such as Accelerated Reader (AR) which allow teachers, parents and students themselves to track what they are reading and how much they are reading. Be aware: AR and other reading programmes are subject to very mixed reviews from the teachers who have implemented them.

---

4   See Institute of Education, Reading for Pleasure, and Attainment in Maths, Vocabulary and Spelling. Research Briefing No. 106 (2014). Available at: http://eprints.ioe.ac.uk/18836/1/RB106_Reading_for_Pleasure_Sullivan.pdf.

Whether you choose a package, create your own bespoke system or prefer to give students autonomy, you must consider the strengths and weakness of extended silent reading. I have witnessed its benefits first hand: it can develop and support a whole-school reading culture; it can offer proficient readers time and encouragement; it can encourage the quiet study habits that are beneficial for future academic success. But it is far from perfect. Weak readers can be left to embed poor reading skills. Some uninterested students learn to feign reading or will choose books far below their ability level. Many children need support and guidance.

At the moment, there is little empirical evidence to support the claim that silent reading programmes are effective in improving reading standards. However, having seen DEAR in action in the two schools in which I have worked, I am cautiously optimistic about its long-term potential. Whatever the evidence shows, shared silent reading approaches help to communicate to our students how much we value the act of reading.

Daniel Willingham has surveyed the evidence on programmes that support reading for pleasure. He makes five suggestions:[5]

♦ Students need at least a twenty-minute reading period.

♦ Students must freely choose what they read.

♦ Students must have ready access to a good number of books.

♦ Students should have some opportunity to feel a sense of community through reading.

♦ The teacher should be actively teaching.

You may also find the following approaches useful:

♦ Make reading a routine by ring-fencing time for it – and sticking to it!

---

5 Willingham, *Raising Kids Who Read*, pp. 172–173.

- Insist that all students carry a book with them and provide lesson time to visit the school library to exchange and renew books. Sanction those without a book.

- Talk about and recommend books with enthusiasm. Tell students about the books you are reading and provide time for students to have structured discussions about books.

- Give students short tasks to complete after reading. This could be filling in a reading journal. If time is at a premium, choose just one student to say something interesting about their book at the end of the session. This builds in accountability. All students know that they could be asked, so know they cannot 'zone out' during DEAR.

- Ensure that alternative support strategies are in place for weak and reluctant readers.

- Build up a strong relationship with the school librarian. A good librarian can be the difference between the success or failure of silent reading systems.

2. Shared oral reading

Reading at secondary school is too often a silent, individual process. Only by hearing each child read aloud can you assess reading capability and work out how to help.

The most manageable way to achieve this is by expecting each and every child to participate in whole-class reading. Many teachers are reluctant to enforce this – and for good reason. Might a student's faltering reading break the spell of a text? Does the anxiety created by having to read out loud have a negative impact on learning? Does the time taken to switch between students waste valuable lesson time? Does the experience of having to read out loud damage the esteem of weaker readers?

All are valid concerns but all can be sidestepped:

- ◆ Choose texts for shared reading that are on a level with, or just above, the capability of the group. If the text contains too much complex vocabulary or unfamiliar grammatical structures, read it yourself.

- ◆ Make reading aloud an expectation from the first lesson you have with a new class. Build a culture of trust and support by gently insisting that peers are sensitive to one another.

- ◆ Switch from reader to reader with a quick, simple script, such as: "Imran, can you start ... Thank you, Imran. Lois ... Thank you, Lois. James ..."

- ◆ Ensure that success becomes inevitable. Give weaker and less confident readers shorter and less complex passages. Do the opposite for your stronger readers.

- ◆ Be human and use your professional discretion. Some students have debilitating anxiety, other mental health conditions or speech impediments; others have fundamental literacy gaps. Utilise support staff and teaching assistants to provide reading aloud opportunities for these students.

3. Shared independent reading

In shared independent reading all students read the same text, only this time on their own. It is important that this happens regularly. Although teachers and students should frequently read out loud, this should not become the sole form of reading. When this happens, some children become so accustomed to listening that they read very little on their own. This is why shared independent reading should be planned for as often as you can – in most lessons if possible.

- ◆ Take length and difficulty into consideration. If the text is hard, give out shorter passages to read.

♦ Avoid talking over the reading and insist upon silence. Children read at different speeds so allow time for this. Ask them to provide a non-verbal signal to show that they are finished, such as turning over the book. Be wary of the ultra-quick 'readers' who will try to skim over the tricky bits!

♦ Check understanding as soon as they have finished. A list of quick tasks or questions that every child must complete is very useful. Make sure that the early tasks check understanding and the later tasks provoke deeper analysis. The first might be, "Write down three things the character does in this extract," whereas the last could be, "How has the writer created empathy for the character?" By expecting a short written answer you build in the expectation that everyone must read to complete the tasks. (Share the tasks after they have finished reading, not before. You do not want the questions to influence how your students read the text in the first instance.)

♦ Go through the answers to the questions with the whole class. In this way, weaker readers do not miss out on any vital information they may have failed to spot or not understood.

2. Process It

How do I get my students to develop their ideas about texts?

Professor Rob Coe has distilled a wealth of cognitive science research into one simple sentence: "Learning happens when people have to think hard."[6] When we have to grapple with a concept, turning it upside down and back to front as if it

---

6   Robert Coe, Improving Education: A Triumph of Hope Over Experience. Inaugural lecture, Durham University, 18 June 2013. Available at: http://www.cem.org/attachments/publications/ImprovingEducation2013.pdf.

were a Rubik's Cube, we are more likely to transfer it to long-term memory. This kind of deep thought also paves the way towards becoming a confident, knowledgeable and critical reader – good readers don't just take on new knowledge, they deliberate on it too. It is important that English teachers differentiate between two related processes: the mechanics of reading itself, and the analysis and interpretation of what has been read.

What is it about literature that young people should be thinking about in the first place? Most teachers and exam boards would probably settle for a list of foundational, intersecting concepts that looks something like this:

♦ Language and linguistic devices

♦ Characterisation

♦ Form and structure

♦ Contextual features

♦ Authorial intention

These are ways of seeing texts – toolboxes that spill over into each other. A child's proficiency in using them should strengthen and crystallise as she moves through the curriculum from text to text.

So where do we start? Should we cover every concept in every text, or should we narrow down to two or three in every text? It is a hard question, but I would argue for depth over breadth. In other words, a handful of concepts in each text for very close teaching and assessment. Over time, we should expect to widen this, allowing students more autonomy as they weave together the concepts.

How do we ensure that students are thinking hard about their reading? When possible, deep processing tasks should follow whole-class reading (once basic understanding is secure). This can work on a micro-scale, after reading a short section of text or a chapter, or on a macro-scale, after reading a complete work or series of shorter texts (such as a poetry anthology). Deep processing tasks should also be used to encourage students to think hard about the factual information you give them – contextual knowledge, author biographies and critical interpretations of texts.

Deep thinking can be prompted and encouraged in many ways. Examples include well-structured paired discussions, extended writing, reorganising and categorising information into different forms, reshaping an abstract idea into a visual image and forming connections between new information and prior knowledge. Indeed, the processes of self-explanation (explaining to yourself why something is true) and elaboration (linking new knowledge to existing knowledge) are essential strategies for embedding something in long-term memory.[7]

However, by far the most useful arrows in the English teacher's quiver are questions. The following table provides an exhaustive list of question templates that help students to think about literature. These questions usually lead to focused, accurate and interesting responses. They are designed to be adapted according to the text you are reading.

---

7   See John Dunlosky, Katherine A. Rawson, Elizabeth J. Marsh, Mitchell J. Nathan and Daniel T. Willingham, Improving Students' Learning with Effective Learning Techniques: Promising Directions from Cognitive and Educational Psychology, *Psychological Science in the Public Interest* 14(1) (2013): 4–58. Available at: http://www.indiana.edu/~pcl/rgoldsto/courses/dunloskyimprovinglearning.pdf.

Language and linguistic devices

1   Which words/phrases/sentences/techniques are used to imply that ____?

2   The writer uses the word/phrase/sentence/technique ____. What does this suggest about ____?

3   Can you find two examples of ____? Which is the most interesting? Why?

4   How does the word/phrase/sentence/technique ____ suggest that ____?

5   The writer uses the word/phrase/sentence/technique ____. Why do you think he/she uses ____ rather than ____?

6   What do we usually associate with ____? What might the writer have been implying about ____ by using this word?

7   What feelings are usually connoted by ____? How do you think these images help the reader to ____?

Characterisation

1   What would you do if you were in the same situation as the character? Would you have behaved similarly or differently? Why?

2   What attributes and qualities best describe the character? Where have we seen evidence to support this?

3   What changes has the character undergone? Why have these changes happened? How do these changes transform the reader's opinion of that character?

4   What is the character's hierarchical position in relation to the other characters in the book? Does this change depending on how we measure it?

5   Is the reader positioned for or against the character? How does this reinforce the writer's view about ____?

8 Where have we seen the writer use _____ before? Why do you think the writer has chosen to use it again?

9 The writer uses _____. Why do you think he/she chose to use this technique at this point in the text?

10 What kind of imagery do we see in the text? How does this help the reader to understand _____?

6 Does the character conform to, or break, the social conventions of the time/place being written about? What evidence from the text supports this?

7 Does the writer use the character to embody or symbolise any attitudes/ideas/central conflicts?

8 How might two readers respond differently to the character and their actions? On what aspects might they agree and disagree?

9 What do we learn about _____ from reading about this character?

10 How would the story function without that character? What would be lost from the story?

Form and structure

1. Can you summarise the sequence of events/ideas in the text?

2. What does _____ at the start of the text make the reader think/feel/believe about _____?

3. What does _____ at the end of the text leave the reader feeling about _____?

4. Why do you think the writer chose to place _____ before _____?

5. What are the major differences between the start and the end of the text? What do these imply about _____?

6. What kind of narrative device is employed? How could you describe the 'voice' of the narrator? Why do you think the writer chose to use this device? How does it differ from other texts you have read?

7. How are the internal structures of the book (paragraphs and chapters) organised? Why do you think the writer made these decisions?

Contextual features

1. What does _____ tell us about what it would have been like to have lived in the time and place in which the text is set?

2. Which parts of the text can you connect to your prior knowledge of the text's context? What factors from the writer's biography may have influenced aspects of the story?

3. What aspects of the writer's contemporary society was he/she supportive and/or critical of?

4. Do you believe that the writer created an accurate portrayal of the time in question? Were any aspects exaggerated or underplayed? Why do you think the writer chose to do this?

5. What are the differences between how _____ would have been received in the writer's time and how it is received today?

8 Where does _____ change? How does this affect the reader's attitude towards _____ ?

6 How does the text compare to other works from that period/by the same writer? How does it compare to works that came before and after?

Authorial intention

1 Who were/are the writer's target audience? How do you know this?

2 What was the writer's main purpose in writing the text?

3 What is the writer's attitude towards _____ ?

4 What do you believe the writer wanted the reader to feel about _____ ?

5 How far do you agree with the writer's attitude towards _____ ?

6 What do you think the writer wanted to teach the reader about the human condition?

7 If the writer could be with us today, what do you think he/she would have thought about _____ ?

8 If _____ was to change, how might it change the reader's attitude to _____ ?

9 What are the strengths and weaknesses of the writer's argument about _____ ?

Here are some examples:

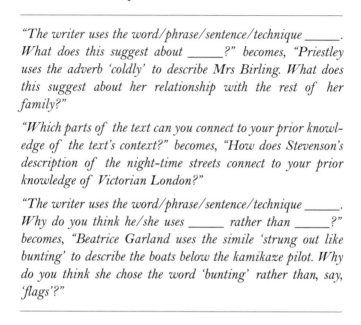

> *"The writer uses the word/phrase/sentence/technique _____.*
> *What does this suggest about _____?" becomes, "Priestley*
> *uses the adverb 'coldly' to describe Mrs Birling. What does*
> *this suggest about her relationship with the rest of her*
> *family?"*
>
> *"Which parts of the text can you connect to your prior knowl-*
> *edge of the text's context?" becomes, "How does Stevenson's*
> *description of the night-time streets connect to your prior*
> *knowledge of Victorian London?"*
>
> *"The writer uses the word/phrase/sentence/technique _____.*
> *Why do you think he/she uses _____ rather than _____?"*
> *becomes, "Beatrice Garland uses the simile 'strung out like*
> *bunting' to describe the boats below the kamikaze pilot. Why*
> *do you think she chose the word 'bunting' rather than, say,*
> *'flags'?"*

While the templates can be used to guide students in developing their own questions, they are most useful as a tool for teachers to design question sequences that lead to verbal or written responses.[8]

There are plenty of other fun and inventive ways to get students processing. After finishing Mark Haddon's novel, *The Curious Incident of the Dog in the Night-Time*, English teacher Caroline Mortlock gave her students four visual symbols that related to themes and ideas from the text: a heart, a car, an eye and a list of prime numbers. In groups of four, the students each took a quarter of a large sheet of paper to explore the significance of each image in writing, talking through their thinking as they wrote.

---

8 See my blog post on this: Question Templates – An Approach to Improving Analysis, *Reflecting English* (2 September 2016). Available at: https:// reflectingenglish.wordpress.com/2016/09/02/ question-templates-an-approach-to-improving-analysis/.

Alex Quigley writes of an ingenious way of helping students to think about the characters of a novel by connecting each to an item in their pencil case.[9] I enjoy asking my classes to find ways of connecting characters to a randomly chosen, unrelated image. For example, I might reveal an image taken from the Internet – a sun setting over a city, for instance – and ask the class to find a symbolic link to a character from the text we are reading. By encouraging them to apply their knowledge in flexible ways, these tasks help students to secure and strengthen their learning.

This strategy comes with an important caveat. Not all reading needs to be processed deeply and hyper-analysed to the nth degree. Young people need to read with breadth as well as depth. It's important to show students that people read 'just because', not just because we have to study a text to pass an exam. Fill your lessons with poetry, short stories and interesting newspaper articles; immerse your students in words for their own sake. Taking a five-minute detour to read something totally unrelated to today's lesson is unlikely to have a negative effect on learning. Not only can this approach foster a love of and curiosity about reading, but it can also build up the range of words, concepts, facts and ideas that students are exposed to at a faster rate.

3. Retain It

How can I prevent my students from forgetting everything I teach them?

The argument about the value of academic knowledge is one that will keep people busy for centuries. On a pragmatic level, our students need to remember what they have read so that they can pass their exams. On a socio-political level, our

---

9   Alex Quigley, *The Confident Teacher: Developing Successful Habits of Mind, Body and Pedagogy* (Abingdon: Routledge, 2016), p. 188.

students need to gain the cultural capital that will allow them to access – and challenge – the dominant power structures of the world. On a personal level, our students need the universal knowledge that literature provides to guide them as they travel along life's often tortuous pathways.

Forgetting – or at least the difficulty students have in storing and retrieving knowledge – is an inevitable part of learning. Many Year 11 students still struggle to tell a metaphor from a simile or a verb from an adverb, despite the fact that they have sat through many lessons where they have been 'taught' these concepts. Students need to be able to recall text-specific knowledge – quotations, events, critical vocabulary and interpretations and contextual facts. And they also need to be able to recall portable, transferable knowledge – literary conventions, linguistic and structural terminology and grammatical concepts.

There are two practical ways that we can help our students to retain content, both supported by a wealth of evidence from cognitive science.[10] The first is to space out practice so that students keep returning to the same material. The second, known as retrieval practice, is to repeatedly test them on this material. The act of retrieving something from memory strengthens connections, making it easier to remember the next time. The strategies that follow are informed by these two principles.

♦ **Pause lessons.** At Durrington High School, the English department have activated the spacing effect by time-tabling an hour per fortnight for lessons that revisit previously studied texts. These lessons are split between retrieval practice (testing students on quotes, concepts and vocabulary) and the promotion of deeper understanding of sophisticated ideas and interpretations. For instance, when revising *An Inspector Calls*, teachers might start by using a range of retrieval tasks and follow this

---

10 See Dunlosky et al., Improving Students' Learning with Effective Learning Techniques.

with an exploration of one aspect of the play – for example, Priestley's use of different theories of time.

♦ **Memory platforms**. Beginning lessons with a review task is a hallmark of effective teaching.[11] Low-stakes quizzes work brilliantly. A good trick is to mix questions that look back to the previous lesson with questions that look back much further. If you are studying a Shakespeare play, ask students to recall not only the scene you looked at last lesson, but also the scene you looked at last week and a relevant idea about a poem studied at the beginning of the year.

The quizzes could be designed like this:

Q1–Q3: Retrieve key knowledge from last lesson.

Q4: Retrieve key knowledge from last week.

Q5: Retrieve key knowledge from last term.

Q6: Retrieve key knowledge from last lesson and connect it to knowledge from last term.

Not only should these questions test factual knowledge, but they should also make students think about semantic meaning. Consider the difference between these two questions: "Which year was *An Inspector Calls* written in?" and "What is significant about the year that *An Inspector Calls* was written in?" The second question provokes recall *and* deep processing.

♦ **Selection-box questions.** Dropping in random short questions on previous content is a useful habit (as suggested in the 'Go intertextual' strategy in Chapter 2). Whenever you are putting together a list of questions, pop in a couple of wildcards to keep your students on their toes. Even more effective is to create questions that forge links between texts – for example, "Mr Birling refuses to listen to the Inspector's warning. How does Scrooge's response to the ghosts make him a very

---

11 See Rosenshine, Principles of Instruction.

different character from Birling?" These are crackerjack questions: they compel the answerer to make connections, to think carefully about meaning and to retrieve previous content.

♦ **Quiz apps and online platforms.** There are plenty of apps available for free that allow students to practise in their own time. Quizlet lets you create digital flashcards, is sublimely simple to use and can be accessed on desktops and mobile devices. Memrise, a quiz app, is particularly useful for vocabulary definitions and memorising key words in quotations.

♦ **Flashcards**. Flashcards mean that students can test themselves – and each other – quickly and receive immediate feedback. They are especially useful for quotation learning.

♦ **Connection tasks.** Give students lists of key words – characters, themes, concepts – and ask them to create visual–spatial organisers that explore the links between them. Then pair them up and ask them to explain and elaborate on their decisions to each other, tracing the connections on the organisers as they go.

♦ **Self-quizzing.** Ask students to create their own quizzes and encourage them to test themselves in their own time.

♦ **Essay plans.** Planning essays means retrieving knowledge and connecting it. It is more efficient to spend a lesson planning answers to a number of essay questions than it is to write an answer to one question in full.

♦ **Mix it up.** There are an endless array of retrieval tasks you could set. It is important that students are encouraged to revise in a range of formats that give them lots of exposure to content. It is no good achieving 100% on a quiz app test but then forgetting everything in the alien environment of the exam hall.

♦ **Writing practice.** Retrieval is only a means to an end. The task of shaping knowledge into an extended written response is a more complex one. Our students will need regular and repeated practice to do this, especially in the lead up to terminal exams.

Reflective Questions

♦ Do you actively support the development of your students' independent reading habits?

♦ Are your students immersed in the study of literature so that they think deeply and independently about what they have read?

♦ Do you help your students to improve their memory of what they have read by directing them towards evidence-informed revision strategies like spacing and retrieval practice?

Chapter 5
Challenging Writing

The good, the bad and the ugly

Brian's mixed-ability Year 8 class have been studying crime stories and it is now time to write their own. He has decided that he wants to make this a challenging and open-ended task and so he gives them carte blanche to write as they would like. The class love this idea; Brian has never seen them so motivated.

After three lessons of feverish writing, the time comes for Brian to look through their work. In truth, he has never been more disappointed. James' effort, for instance, is a three-page 'thriller' composed almost entirely of mockney gangster dialogue and no paragraphs, whereas Isobel has written a crime mystery with a cast of over ten undeveloped characters, all of whom share names, strangely enough, with her best friends in school. Brian sifts through the class's efforts in ever deepening despair until he comes to Muhammad's story – a brilliant, psychologically astute internal monologue written from the viewpoint of a would-be murderer.

This scenario exposes the challenges we face when setting up a writing task, especially an extended one. Despite Brian's willingness to challenge his class, and despite their enthusiastic reception, the written results were variable.

One cause of the poor quality of James' and Isobel's work was a lack of guidance and scaffolding; another was task parameters that were too wide and too loose. Most English teachers are passionate about fostering creativity and artistic expression in young people, but this well-meaning approach can have a flip side too. All the time James and Isobel were writing, they were not becoming better writers; they were consolidating bad habits that will become increasingly hard to budge in the future.

Constraints and parameters are not the enemy of the imagination. Fiction writer Neil Gaiman apparently sees it like this: "Parameters are the things you bounce off to create art." This is even supported by recent research evidence which shows that when children are given constraints on a poetry writing task their work becomes more creative.[1] In short, fewer alternatives allow for greater exploration – a maxim that should be applied to all student writing tasks.

But what about Muhammad, the boy who wrote with such intensity and panache? Even streamed groups contain a range of abilities, so a flexible approach that leaves some room for creative autonomy is important.

A more structured approach with clear parameters should not mean that children do less writing. Over time, students should write increasingly developed and detailed pieces that help them to build up their stamina and their writing 'muscles'. Ideally, most English lessons should include some form of independent writing, if only for a few minutes. A short task can still be a challenging one.

---

1 See Catrinel Haught-Tromp, The Green Eggs and Ham Hypothesis: How Constraints Facilitate Creativity, *Psychology of Aesthetics, Creativity, and the Arts* (2016). Available at: http://www.rider.edu/sites/default/files/docs/ tromp_haught-tromp_PACA_2016.pdf.

The difficulty in assessing writing and giving useful feedback causes another problem. Look at this sentence written by a Year 9 student:

Coldly silent and still, the ancient, decrepit man's body lay dead on the rigid, unforgiving ground.

While the grammar is accurate and the descriptive adjectives are relevant, the sentence is awkward and over-inflated. A direct sentence can be more powerful, even if it 'ticks off' fewer boxes on an assessment rubric:

He lay dead.

Writing, therefore, cannot only be understood in measurable terms. It is easy to count the vivid verbs and the ellipses in a piece of work, but these do not tell us whether it is great writing. A writer's sense of voice, the logical development of ideas and the awareness of audience are crucial, but hard to break down into teachable chunks of knowledge. In the work of expert writers, the whole is always greater than the sum of its parts. And because true quality is so difficult to explain, part of the teaching solution, once again, lies in the challenge and richness of the texts in which our students are immersed. Perhaps our best hope is that they will subconsciously transfer this flair to their own written work.

Finally, a challenging writing task is not just a hard one; it is an achievable one. It should give every child every chance of producing a rigorous, high-quality final product.

1. Balance Content and Genre

How do I teach students to develop their writing in depth and detail?

In my first few years as an English teacher, I would overlook the amount of content knowledge my students needed before writing. When I was teaching rhetorical writing, for example, my class would read some famous speeches and I would ask them to identify rhetorical devices and their effects. I would then ask them to replicate the structure, style and techniques they had learnt about in their own writing. They would choose a topic (e.g. euthanasia or gun laws in the United States), research it and then write the speech. Quite often the final work was shallow and poorly argued.

In recent years, I have taken a different tack. This has involved dedicating more lesson time to the direct teaching of the topic the class will be writing about. A recent unit on writing a speech about child poverty involved dedicating time to explicitly teaching the class about child poverty in the UK (with the help of broadsheet articles and an excellent BBC documentary) and less time teaching generic speech writing techniques. Often English teachers expect all students to build their topic knowledge by setting independent research as homework. Unfortunately, this task disadvantages those students who do not have the research skills and background knowledge to find useful and credible facts and ideas.

My new approach led to better speeches which contained developed arguments and well-researched evidence. The most able in the class were given the option of a more challenging spin on the same kind of task: "Would a more equal world be a better world?" Here they could weave in their wider background knowledge.

Because creative writing is imaginative it creates a different problem. What we can imagine is based on the direct and indirect experiences we have had (i.e. through wider reading) and what we already know about the world. This is why disadvantaged students who have less general knowledge than their peers often struggle with open-ended stimuli – they do not have well-developed schemas to fall back on.

The solution is to link creative writing, when possible, to the texts that the class are currently studying. That way, there is a knowledge base for all to work from. Good tasks might include:

♦ Write the character's internal monologue, detailing how they feel during chapter 5.

♦ Imagine you were an extra character in this scene. Explain it from your standpoint.

♦ Write an alternative ending to the chapter/book.

♦ Describe somebody you know, or a place you know, using the same style and technique as the writer.

♦ Perhaps your high-flyers could take a different spin on the task: describe Macbeth as if you were Charles Dickens, or write a satirical version of this chapter.

For shorter writing tasks, like practising grammatical constructions or rhetorical figures of speech, simple stimuli (such as pictures and short clips of film) can be very useful. When you do choose to use a non-literary stimulus, make sure you spend a lot of time planning with the class so that background knowledge gaps are addressed beforehand.

To sum up: make sure children know a lot about a topic before they start writing about it!

2. Start Easy, Finish Hard

How can I motivate my students to attempt difficult writing tasks?

A central tenet of the 'Making Every Lesson Count' books is that teachers should avoid setting completely different work for different students according to their starting points. The alternative is to set a high level of challenge for all, and then find the best way of helping all students to reach this goal, regardless of ability. While it is important that every student is expected to complete every writing task, there should always be some form of extra support available and a way that some students can develop the task even further.

Many children find it hard to start a piece of writing, but once they get pen to paper things pick up quickly. There is a useful rule: tasks should be easy to start, but hard to do well.

Thankfully, experienced English teachers usually have a number of launch-pad tricks up their sleeves:

♦ **Starter sentences and phrases.** Not only do these give students something to latch on to, but they also allow you to subtly introduce the tone and style in which you wish them to continue.

♦ **Shared writing.** Creating a class model for the first few sentences always works a treat. You start with convergence and leave the students to diverge independently.

♦ **Class discussion and notes.** Discuss possible ways of starting and take notes on the board which will then act as an aide-memoire. It is a very simple way to have your high-starting students support your low-starters without drawing attention to the difference between them.

♦ **Student examples.** If the class have started writing and some are struggling, choose a good example to read out loud or, even better, display it on the board with a visualiser or a photo uploaded from your smartphone to a cloud storage application on your computer.

In the long term, students will need to stop relying on your help, which is why a set of stock prompts for everyone to memorise can prove useful. For creative writing, it could be, "Start with a description of a sound" or "Start at a distance and close in". In rhetorical writing, "Start with the words *Only yesterday*" or "Start by complimenting your audience". Remind the class that these emergency fall backs are only to be used in a case of writer's block – you do not want to find yourself marking fifty persuasive speeches that begin with the hackneyed line, "Imagine a world where ..." as I once did!

3. Emulate the Literary Greats

How do I challenge my students to write like experts?

One of the best ways to help young people understand how language works is to ask them to emulate the work of great writers. This is one of those tasks that helps improve aspects of both reading and writing.

First, take a section from a text you are reading. Choose one that perfectly highlights the writer's craft, such as this description of Scrooge's dwelling from Stave 1 of Charles Dickens' *A Christmas Carol*:

Scrooge took his melancholy dinner in his usual melancholy tavern; and having read all the newspapers, and beguiled the rest of the evening with his banker's-book, went home to bed. He lived in chambers which had once belonged to his deceased partner. They were a gloomy suite of rooms, in a lowering pile of building up a yard, where it had so little business to be, that one could scarcely help fancying it must have run there when it was a young house, playing at hide-and-seek with other houses, and forgotten the way out again. It was old enough now, and dreary enough, for nobody lived in it but Scrooge, the other rooms being all let out as offices. The yard was so dark that even Scrooge, who knew its every stone, was fain to grope with his hands. The fog and frost so hung about the black old gateway of the house, that it seemed as if the Genius of the Weather sat in mournful meditation on the threshold.

Second, guide your class towards the writer's key language, structure and style choices. Here it could be:

- ♦ The use of repetition to intensify the soporific mood: *melancholy* and *enough*.

- The use of pathetic fallacy: "They were a gloomy suite of rooms."

- The use of symbolism to represent Dickens' attitudes: the *dark* is Scrooge's cruelty, the *fog* his moral blindness.

- The use of personification: "a young house, playing at hide-and-seek".

Next, decide on the task. Perhaps they could describe the house as if it belonged to Scrooge's Christmas-loving alter-ego, or perhaps they could describe the house of a twenty-first century Scrooge. There are plenty of possible permutations. The focus of tasks like this are that the students should maintain the writer's techniques but apply them differently to the new context.

There is one limitation to this excellent strategy: do not forget that young people also still require time and space to develop their personal style.

4. Go Greek

What is the simplest method for encouraging teenagers to write with genuine flair?

Unfortunately, there are no silver bullets, but at least this strategy has stood the test of time.[2] At school, Shakespeare and his contemporaries were required to rote learn hundreds of rhetorical devices which dated back to the Ancient Greeks. These days, it would be foolhardy to expect students to learn this many, but there is no reason why they should not master the most useful.

---

2 Sam Leith's *You Talkin' to Me? Rhetoric from Aristotle to Obama* (London: Profile Books, 2012) and Mark Forsyth's *Elements of Eloquence: How to Turn the Perfect English Phrase* (London: Icon Books, 2016) are both must-reads for all teachers of English.

Take *anaphora*, for instance – the repetition of a word or phrase at the beginning of successive phrases, clauses or lines. It is so simple to teach, yet it imbues even the most pedestrian of paragraphs with a rolling, gathering rhythm, momentum and sense of anticipation. The trick to teaching rhetorical devices is that they need not only be applied to persuasive writing; they readily transfer to almost all genres, even essay writing.

If you desire real mastery, you could do the following:

♦ Introduce a few at the start of the year and spend at least twenty minutes, if not a full lesson, on each.

♦ Show lots of examples and have students practise using them in isolation.

♦ Insist that students rote learn their definitions for homework. Test their understanding regularly across the year.

♦ Expect students to recognise them in the texts you read.

♦ Expect students to use them in their writing.

Here are seven of the best that I have tried and tested in my classroom.

Technique	Description	Example
Anadiplosis	The repetition of a word or phrase that ends one clause at the beginning of the next. (It means to 'double back'.)	"The love of wicked men converts to fear; that fear to hate, and hate turns one or both to worthy danger and deserved death." (Shakespeare, *Richard II*)
Anaphora	The repetition of a word or phrase at the beginning of successive phrases, clauses or lines.	"We shall not flag or fail. We shall go on to the end. We shall fight in France." (Churchill)
Antistrophe	The repetition of the same word or phrase at the end of successive clauses (the opposite to anaphora).	"When I was a child, I spake as a child, I understood as a child, I thought as a child: but when I became a man I put away childish things." (1 Corinthians 13:11)
Antithesis	The contrast of words or ideas.	"The well-bred contradict other people. The wise contradict themselves." (Oscar Wilde)

Technique	Description	Example
Chiasmus	Pairs of words ordered in an a–b–b–a formation.	"When the going gets tough, the tough get going." (Billy Ocean)
Diacope	The repetition of a word or phrase with some intervening words.	"My name is Bond, James Bond."
Isocolon	The placing together of sentences that are equal in length, structure and rhythm.	"Morning has broken, like the first morning, Blackbird has spoken, like the first bird." (Traditional hymn)

Reflective Questions

♦ Do you immerse your students in the topic they will write about as well as in the generic features of good writing?

♦ Are your students developing the habit of emulating the stylistic features of great writing?

♦ Do you find ways to make challenging writing tasks achievable?

♦ Do you challenge your students by directing them towards challenging writing devices, such as Ancient Greek rhetorical constructions?

Chapter 6

Explaining Writing

The assessment rubric

Tabitha's English teacher is teaching her class to use sensory language in descriptive writing. The lesson starts with the sharing of a challenging learning objective: to be able to use sensory language convincingly and originally in a piece of descriptive writing. Tabitha copies the words down neatly, even if she does not quite understand what they mean. Once the class has identified all the sights, sounds, smells, tastes and sensations one might experience on a trip to the beach, a descriptive writing task is set. Tabitha's teacher shares some success criteria based on the school's Key Stage 3 English assessment rubric, which is helpfully presented on the board as a reminder:

Excellent writing will include convincing and original sensory descriptions.

Secure writing will include effective and interesting sensory descriptions.

Developing writing will include thoughtful sensory descriptions.

Foundation writing will include some attempt to use sensory descriptions.

Her teacher discusses what these might mean with the class. Tabitha listens carefully and starts writing. In her piece, she describes the sounds of the waves and the ice cold sensation of the wind on her narrator's face.

Her descriptive writing is no better or worse than it has ever been.

The oversight Tabitha's teacher has made is to share the language of assessment criteria without using examples. Daisy Christodoulou has dubbed this the 'adverb problem'. Adverbs and adjectives like 'convincing', 'thoughtful' and 'fairly' are loaded with subjectivity. Unless they are accompanied by concrete examples, their meaning lies in the eye of the beholder.[1] Their ambiguity means that they are useless in helping students to gain a grasp of the quality they should be aiming for.

It is infuriatingly difficult to explain to another person what makes a piece of writing a 'good' piece of writing. Although we might resort to sharing bullet-pointed lists of the features we would expect to see, these often come up short. Something feels missing. Proficient writers rely on their tacit knowledge – that is, the vast stores of expertise they have accumulated over many years. If a tightrope walker or master chess player were to sit down with you and explain the tricks of their trades, it is highly unlikely that the very next day you would be tiptoeing on a thread across a precipitous drop or giving Garry Kasparov a run for his money at the World Chess Championship. The same is true for writing. Genuine skill takes many years to master; it cannot be distilled into sound bites of advice.

---

1 Daisy Christodoulou, The Adverb Problem, *The Wing to Heaven* (24 November 2013). Available at: https://thewingtoheaven.wordpress.com/2013/11/24/the-adverb-problem/.

Thankfully, by improving the quality of our explanations, we can begin to reverse some of these problems.

1. Know Your Grammar

How can I find a common language to talk about writing?

Like every English teacher, I despair at the punctuation errors my students make: the missing capital letters, the frivolous commas, the semicolons thrown in with wanton abandon. Sometimes this is caused by bad habits or lack of effort; at other times the cause lies in students' lack of secure grammar knowledge. Endless reminders to "Use a capital letter at the start of a sentence and a full stop at the end" or to "Make sure that every sentence has a main verb" fall on deaf ears because the child does not understand what a sentence or verb is in the first place.

Two of the most important underlying grammar concepts are word classes (noun, verb, adjective, adverb, etc.) and the three sentence types (simple, compound and complex). Once these terms are truly mastered, you suddenly have a shared language to explain and discuss how language works. You can say to a student that "Even though it was dark" is an ungrammatical sentence fragment because it is not a complete thought – it is a subordinate clause that has not been attached to a main clause to form a compound or complex sentence. The benefit of teaching grammar is that it gives us a shared meta-language for explanation. It also helps us to explain and discuss writers' language choices with far greater clarity – for example, "What effect is conveyed by this periodic sentence – a sentence that uses several subordinate clauses before revealing the main clause?"

Of course, studying English is much more than grammatical acrobatics. Meaning matters. Nevertheless, a secure understanding of grammar foundations allows for far greater clarity of language discussion. And besides, is the study of the ever-evolving systems and structures of our vast and exuberant language not worthy of attention in its own right?

How to teach grammar is one of the most controversial questions in English teaching at the moment. There are two schools of thought: teach it in a contextualised and 'meaningful' way or teach it through decontextualised drills.

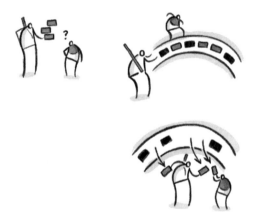

Debra Myhill's research has found that contextualised grammar teaching can lead to an improvement in students' achievement in writing (although the reliability of these results is contested by some). She argues that there are three key principles at work in good grammar teaching: students must make links and connections between grammatical choices and the genre the text is written in; students should look at examples and patterns, even if they do not remember the meta-language; and students must be given time to discuss the grammar choices they are making.[2] In other words,

---

2   A useful video that sums up Myhill's approach can be found at: https://www.youtube.com/watch?v=VXr09X86K20.

grammar should be taught through genre – for instance, how persuasive writing makes use of a range of sentence constructions.

In decontextualised grammar teaching, the teacher ignores genre and teaches the grammatical concept in isolation. This time, the sentence structures would be taught without reference to persuasive writing. The advantage of this approach is that it puts less strain on a child's working memory, leaving them able to pay attention to grammar alone. This is said to promote greater accuracy. The trouble with decontextualised grammar, however, is that students often struggle to transfer the learning into their everyday writing. We see this when a student performs well in a lesson on the use of the semicolon, but then misuses them in his next piece of extended writing.

So what's the solution? I prefer a third, hybrid option. Lessons – or parts of lessons – should be dedicated to the isolated, explicit teaching of key grammar concepts. These should be very carefully sequenced because grammar knowledge is hierarchical – a lesson on how to use commas is pretty useless if you do not know how complex sentences work. However, students should also be guided in applying this knowledge to the texts they read and write. At this point, Myhill's advice – look for connections, use examples, discuss choices – becomes very useful.

2. Pair Examples with Non-examples

What is the clearest way of explaining the complex technicalities of language?

A golden rule for any explanation about writing is that it should be accompanied by a visible example. That way, a student can concentrate on your teaching point, rather than attempting the impossible feat of holding a series of complete sentences in their working memory at one time.

As you will see below, the more examples you use, the better.

You are teaching your class how to use a semicolon. You start with an empty board and write down (or reveal) this sentence:

Tom was unhappy; Arsenal had lost that day.

You explain the role of the semicolon here. It alerts the reader to the fact that the two main clauses are related to each other: Tom is unhappy because Arsenal have lost – not because his hamster has died, his girlfriend has ditched him or he has had an unfortunate accident on the way to class. At this point, you explain that a semicolon divides two main clauses or two complete thoughts. To be grammatically accurate, each clause – each side of the semicolon – must make sense on its own. You then ask the class why a comma in its place would be ungrammatical (it would lead to a splice sentence) and why a full stop might suggest a slightly different meaning (perhaps Tom's misery was caused by something other than Arsenal's unfortunate defeat).

Next you show a new example sentence:

The tiger is a ferocious predator; it can kill an animal twice its size.

Again, you talk through the semicolon rules, this time asking a few questions to test understanding: "If I wrote the conjunction 'and' before 'it', would the sentence still be grammatical? Can we replace the semicolon with a comma? Would this sentence be acceptable with a full stop between the main clauses?"

Then you display another example:

The winter is the most depressing time of year; the summer is full of joy.

This time you choose Hannah, a girl at the back, to explain how the sentence works, probing her to explain how the rules have been met. You also use this as an opportunity to increase the class's understanding of how and when to use a semicolon – they are pithy dividers of antithetical clauses.

Finally, you show two non-examples (incorrect examples that reveal common errors and misconceptions):

> Julian is my closest friend; and I can never be apart from him.

> Even though I am a Tottenham fan; I have a soft spot for Brighton and Hove Albion.

This time you ask your class to explain to you why these are incorrect and how they could be edited to make them correct.

Eventually, you give your class a list of example sentences – some right, some wrong – to practise independently.

This staged approach, which gradually hands over explanation and thinking, can be used to teach any grammatical or literary device, including notions of aesthetic quality. For instance, you might contrast examples of striking and unusual metaphors with non-examples of trite and clichéd metaphors. Your class could then write and discuss their own metaphors.

A word of warning. Students rarely, if ever, master complex grammar rules after one exposure. You will need to return regularly to the semicolon over weeks, terms and years for true mastery. If you do, you will begin to see your students flourish as they apply them accurately in a range of written contexts.

3. Use Memory Cues

What is the most foolproof way to help students to learn difficult-to-remember content?

When we write we need items of knowledge at our finger-tips: grammar rules, complex spelling rules, punctuation rules and ways to structure paragraphs and full texts; however, much of this is hard to remember.

A time-honoured and evidence-informed strategy to combat this is to use mnemonics. A mnemonic is any device that aids the memory. Rhymes, acronyms, acrostics and visual associations – the stranger, the better! – can all play a role. They provide a memory cue – something tangible on which to hang a memory that makes it easier to retrieve. When I was at school, my English teacher helped me to spell psychology through the silly phrase, 'Phillip Schofield's yellow coat hanger'. This cue is now burnt into my long-term memory.

Below are a few popular examples for pieces of difficult-to-remember writing knowledge. It is best to introduce them at the point of teaching.

Item to be learnt	Memory cue
The spelling of 'necessary'	One collar and two socks.
When to start a new paragraph	TiPToP – Time, Place, Topic, Person.
The difference between 'there' and 'their'	There contains 'here' – a place. Their contains 'i' – an object belonging to a person.

Item to be learnt	Memory cue
The spelling of 'rhythm'	Rhythm Helps Your Two Hips Move.
The difference between 'practice' and 'practise'	Practice is a noun. It has the word 'ice' in it, which is a noun. Practise is a verb. It has the word 'is' in it, which is a verb.
The spelling of 'separate'	There's a rat in separate.

The trick is to invent, collect and share these wonderfully useful tips whenever possible. If you use them regularly, they will stick. Conjuring them up from scratch is a tough and time-consuming task, but a Google search or the online Mnemonic Dictionary can help.[3] Keep a list of them and display them in your classroom. Keep your classes well-oiled by quizzing them regularly.

4. Open the Rulebook

Why do some students seem to ignore the success descriptors I share with them?

In their wonderful book, *Switch: How to Change When Change Is Hard*, Chip and Dan Heath suggest that "what looks like resistance is often a lack of clarity".[4] This may go towards explaining why many young people's writing does not always improve in response to our teaching: they need concise, crystal-clear success criteria.

---

3   See http://mnemonicdictionary.com/.

4   Chip Heath and Dan Heath, *Switch: How to Change When Change Is Hard* (London: Random House, 2011), p. 264.

Have you ever set up a writing task like this?

Right class, here are ten things I want you to do to make this a fantastic essay! (Present slide without giving the class a chance to read it, let alone digest it.)

Now, have a look at your new double-sided placemat of 99 sophisticated connectives. Make sure you don't bend them; I spent three hours lovingly laminating them last night! Use these to link your ideas together … Oh, and before you forget, flick back in your exercise books to the three targets I set you last lesson …

(Two minutes into the written task.) Oh, by the way, I forgot to mention …

Your advice has completely swamped your class and your best intentions have actively worked against you. A better option is to distil your advice down to as few items as possible, using words as clearly and sparingly as you can. The less proficient the writer, the more likely you are to swamp them with too many things to do.

Moreover, woolly success criteria should be replaced by simple, unambiguous rules (as shown in the following table). This reality has taken me many years of heartache to recognise. If this all feels too draconian, remember that intelligent parameters can inspire creativity – even if this feels counter-intuitive.

Success criterion	Rule
Use a varied range of sentence starts, including adverbial phrases and prepositional phrases.	Start every sentence with a different word to make your writing varied and interesting.

Success criterion	Rule
Ensure that all points are fully explored in depth and detail.	Include *at least* four sentences in every paragraph to ensure that points are explored in depth and detail.
Spell almost all ambitious and unusual words correctly.	Circle, check and tick every unusual word so that you have a better chance of spelling it correctly.

Despite the advantages of this approach, danger lurks in the shadows. There is a thin line between helpful parameters and a reductive tick-list approach. Tips for good writing should never sound like a recipe: "Make sure your writing includes four semicolons, three similes, two sentences written in the subjunctive mood and, to top it off, don't forget to stir in an oxymoron."

There is another exciting way to improve the tangibility of your task instructions. That is to stipulate not only the skills students need to show in their writing, but also the effect that these should have on the reader – as in the following examples:

♦ **Sentence.** Write a sentence about an old house, using a colon to introduce something unexpected.

♦ **Paragraph.** Use two complex sentences followed by three simple sentences to capture the beauty of a sunrise.

♦ **Whole text.** Write a five-paragraph formal letter to the prime minister arguing for the abolition of independent schools. In the first paragraph demonstrate your anger, in the second your frustration and in the third your hope.

Be aware: students find these kinds of tasks hard, but they really do make them think about the relationship between purpose and technique. Indeed, the modern obsession with exam rubrics and skill-centric success criteria has meant that teachers often overlook the importance of guiding students towards an intended impact.

And lastly, if you would prefer your students to choose the techniques for themselves, then just stipulate the desired effect:

♦ Describe a female character's movements so the reader feels that she is nursing a terrible secret.

♦ Describe a house in an ominous way so the reader feels that something terrible is about to occur.

♦ Write an argument for/against testing on animals that makes the reader feel both terrible pity and extreme anger.

Ultimately, your aim is to keep the woolly mammoth of abstract success criteria where he belongs: in his icy grave.

Reflective Questions

♦ Do you create a shared language to discuss the mechanics of writing by teaching grammar directly?

♦ Do you help students to avoid common writing errors and misconceptions by immersing them in examples and non-examples?

♦ Are your students developing the habit of creating and using mnemonics to become more accurate writers?

♦ Do you direct students towards concrete and achievable success criteria?

Chapter 7

Modelling Writing

Chalk 'n' talk

Ms Randolf has been teaching English for three years. Her students enjoy her lessons; she loves the subject and she knows it inside out. The trouble is that the quality of her students' writing never quite hits the mark. The quantity is there, the effort is there, but the final product is immature and unambitious. Despite her best efforts, Ms Randolf's classes' writing seems to have hit a glass ceiling. Ms Randolf is frustrated. I know they have more potential, she thinks despairingly, but how do I coax it out?

One morning, Ms Randolf is caught in traffic and arrives late to school with no time to put together her lessons. For the first time in her career she is going to have to improvise. She does her best to disguise her sheer terror.

"Open your books, ladies and gentlemen," she says, feigning confidence. "I'm sorry, but today's going to be a chalk-and-talk lesson. I'm going to write and you're going to copy. Please feel

free to chip in and help me whenever you can. Then you're going to do some writing of your own, independently."

What a fortuitous set of roadworks! Ms Randolf is amazed by the work the students produce later in the lesson.

Ms Randolf has happened upon the powerful effect that modelling can have on student writing. To model writing means to hold a microscope to the mysterious, private experience of a writer who is transforming thoughts into words. By taking the time to show her writing and talk through her decisions, Ms Randolf's unintended approach had a transformational effect on her students' subsequent work.

First we should consider what we mean by modelling. There are two distinct types: working backwards from an excellent model and working forwards towards an excellent model. The first involves revealing a completed end product to the class – a sentence, a paragraph, a full text – and then taking it apart, bit by bit, to investigate the writer's craftsmanship. This could be the work of a literary behemoth, it could be something you have written in advance (perhaps based on a class weakness or a specific learning point) or it could be a good student example. After they have deconstructed it, your class will then attempt to emulate specific features of the work for themselves – remember, *emulate the greats.*

The psychologist K. Anders Ericsson has identified the role of mental representations in the development of expertise in every domain, including writing.[1] A child who appears to be a 'natural writer' is likely to have built well-developed mental representations of what makes good quality writing. By comparing the visible piece he is writing to the conception of quality he holds in his mind, he is able to monitor his progress as he goes and make necessary improvements. The regular building and deconstructing of models helps to build this internal understanding.

---

1   See Ericsson and Pool, *Peak.*

The second approach, stumbled upon by Ms Randolf, is to write 'live' and work towards a model. This has a double advantage: it demonstrates the (often messy) way that a writer creates a text in all its glory *and* provides an excellent example for students to aim for and compare their own work to. If they do not see these examples, then we must rely on a child's mental representation of excellent writing. Inevitably, only those whose writing is already advanced and well-honed will have this.

Despite its turbo-charged potential, many teachers are not confident with 'live writing'. When we decide to write in front of the class, we also open ourselves up to mistakes – we become vulnerable. Another common anxiety in these times of shifting goalposts and new GCSE examinations is that we start to doubt our ability to identify and reproduce excellent work. (If I don't know what a grade 8 or 9 piece of work at GCSE really looks like, how can I model an example?)

Both concerns are understandable but both can be overcome. Like anything, we become better at modelling through practice. It will not always feel safe or smooth; sometimes in the spotlight we will come face to face with the dreaded writer's block ourselves. But the truth is, these experiences are valuable – many of our students feel just like this when we ask them to write. Modelling can lead to heightened empathy for our students – a priceless outcome in its own right. The second problem can be worked through. Excellent writing is always excellent writing. You might be an inexperienced teacher but you are not an inexperienced writer.

A final, more compelling, concern is that modelling stunts and curtails creativity. There is some truth in this argument. Bad modelling can suppress rather than draw out a child's ability, which is why much of this chapter focuses not only on how to model well, but also on obvious pitfalls to avoid.

1. Think of Your Reader

How do I ensure that I model like a real writer?

Writers write for a purpose and an audience. And that audience is rarely a greying, 30-something schoolteacher desperately trying to mark a pile of dog-eared exercise books before this evening's Premier League match kicks off on Sky Sports! It is important that young writers learn to picture and conceptualise their intended reader.

Would horror writer Stephen King start a chapter thinking: Ah, today I would like to show off my ability to use emotive language and a rhetorical question? It is highly unlikely. Instead, he might be thinking, explicitly or implicitly: I want to show this character's arrogance so that the reader feels little sympathy when he becomes the first victim. Or perhaps: I want to unsettle my reader by describing this seemingly innocuous building in an eerie way.

Writers work by choosing the effect they want to achieve and then utilising the strategies and techniques at their fingertips to do this. This is often an unconscious process. To borrow David Didau's phrase, teaching writing is about "making the implicit explicit".[2]

---

2 The subtitle of David Didau's book, *The Secret of Literacy: Making the Implicit Explicit* (Carmarthen: Independent Thinking Press, 2014).

2. Model Short

What is the best way to model the thought processes that go into writing a good sentence?

It is important that children think about the constituent parts of a whole text. We should model short, medium and long texts – in other words, sentences, paragraphs and full texts.

A single sentence offers an intriguing gateway into a writer's world. The beauty of single-sentence modelling is that it allows you to dedicate a lot of time to fine-tuning the very small details. One of my favourite strategies is the 'sentence escalator'. It works like this:

1   Choose a poor sentence in need of a makeover and display it. You could invent this or it could come from a student's work.

2   Show how it can be improved, writing the new version out again underneath the original version.

3   Open it out to the class: what other changes could they make to improve the sentence? Write up the improved version.

4   Continue to improve it as many times as necessary, each time writing down the improvement so that you have a visual record of each draft.

5   Give your students more sentences to work on or ask them to edit something they have already written.

This is an example from a Year 9 class:

♦   Initial sentence: "He's drinking alcohol to calm his nerves."

♦   First improvement: "I am drinking an alcoholic beverage to calm my nerves and calm my desperation to stay alive."

♦ Second improvement: "Trembling in fear, I picked up a bottle of whiskey, while my hand shook."

♦ Third improvement: "Trembling, I grasp a bottle of whiskey, my hand shaking like the boat."

♦ Fourth improvement: "I grasp a bottle of whiskey, my hand juddering."

Along the way many decisions were discussed: the choice of first person narration over third person, the impact of present tense over past tense, the effect of the verbs 'grasp' and 'juddering' over 'picked' and 'shaking' and the importance of showing over telling. It is wonderful how the editing process becomes visual so that children can see that real writers do not just make do with the first idea that comes to mind.

This strategy also works well when showing students how to write in a condensed critical style. English teacher Kate Bloomfield is particularly fond of sleek, single-sentence character summaries. For example: "Over the course of the novella, Dickens takes Scrooge on a journey from solitude and misanthropy to redemption and enlightenment."

A different approach to one-sentence modelling can be found in the work of English teacher and blogger, Chris Curtis, who draws his inspiration from Alan Peat's book *Writing Exciting Sentences*.[3] Chris, with English teachers Anne Williams and Kerry Pulleyn, has developed a series of excellent sentence structures that adept writers employ almost unconsciously as part of their arsenal:[4]

---

3   Alan Peat, *Writing Exciting Sentences: Age 7+* (Biddulph: Creative Educational Press, 2008).

4   See Chris's blog post which includes many other examples: Death to Sentence Stems! Long Live the Sentence Structures! *Learning From My Mistakes: An English Teacher's Blog* (1 February 2014). Available at: http://learningfrommymistakesenglish.blogspot.co.uk/2014/02/death-to-sentence-stems-long-live.html.

Sentence	Example
More, more, more sentence	The more he thought about the answer, the more he noticed the time remaining, the more his future looked dire.
Colons to clarify	There was something not quite right about the bedroom: it was missing a bed.
Distance (closer, nearer, further)/ more sentence	The closer we got to the house, the more I wanted to turn away.
The writer's aside sentence	The exam, as we know, is very difficult. I feel, to be frank, there must be another way.
Adjectives at the start of the sentence	Anxious and dismayed, Gwen sat with the envelope on her lap.
End-loaded sentence – dramatic ending	Beneath the glistening sun and clear blue sky, the birds sung merrily as they sweetly hopped about the grass and pecked for seeds near the murdered girl.
Not only, but also sentence	Not only was she confident and well prepared, but she had also spent the last three weeks revising for this exam.
However after the subject of the sentence	The teachers, however, expected Emma to behave aggressively.

Sentence	Example
Shakespearean I wish I was/ would that I were sentence	Would that I were a ring on her finger.
Repeat and develop ideas sentence	The journey was frustrating and troubling – frustrating in that the bus broke down several times, troubling in that the bus driver had no idea how to operate the vehicle.

A great way to teach these is to share and discuss an example – let's say, the 'colons to clarify' sentence.

A strange hint of something filled his nostrils and made his stomach lurch: it was blood.

Then choose a new context in which to use the sentence:

Lord Capulet's behaviour towards Juliet in Act 3, Scene 5 reveals something very unpleasant about the treatment of daughters in the Elizabethan age: if they chose to openly disobey their fathers they could expect to be treated violently or even disowned.

And, to finish, the students will need to complete a sentence of their own. Perhaps they could describe a food that they particularly dislike, giving the reason after the colon.

3. Model Medium

What is the most effective way to model the writing of a paragraph?

Like sentences, paragraphs should also be modelled. Modelling paragraphs allows us to teach the structure of an idea and the connections between sentences. It works perfectly within the bounds of an hour-long lesson.

Start by sharing a pre-written, labelled example. This taps into what cognitive scientists call the 'worked example effect'. (A worked example is "a step-by-step demonstration of how to perform a task or how to solve a problem".[5])

Here is an example that I used when teaching Alfred, Lord Tennyson's 'The Charge of the Light Brigade':

At the start of 'The Charge of the Light Brigade', Tennyson created a feeling of momentum and energy. We see this in the first three lines of the poem: "Half a league, half a league, Half a league onward …" Here the use of anaphora in the phrase "half a league" helps to convey the sense that the soldiers are moving forward relentlessly, without looking back. Moreover, it helps Tennyson to put across the idea that these men are fearless and courageous defenders of their country, who would charge towards the enemy without a thought for their own lives.

Topic sentence to introduce the main idea you will be discussing.

Quotation from the poem (mentioning which verse it comes from).

An explanation of one (or more) interesting words/phrases from the quotation.

---

5   Ruth C. Clark, Frank Nguyen and John Sweller, *Efficiency in Learning: Evidence-Based Guidelines to Manage Cognitive Load* (San Francisco, CA: Pfeiffer, 2006), p. 190.

> *An explanation of how the quotation shows Tennyson's ideas about the soldiers and/or war.*

First, we picked apart the paragraph. We discussed the role of the topic sentence (something that many students struggle to get to grips with). We discussed why I had chosen the quotation and how to 'zoom in' on the quotation for closer inspection. Finally, we discussed how evidence helps us to interpret a writer's viewpoint.

Next came the best bit: the live writing. I wanted to explore another aspect of Tennyson's poem: how he juxtaposes the brutality of war with the nobility of the soldiers. Because my class had already seen an example, they were well-primed for shared live writing.

When live writing for the first few times, plan a few questions in advance. Write them down if you need to. Here were mine:

♦ What role does the topic sentence play?

♦ How shall we start off our topic sentence?

♦ Where do we go next?

♦ Which quotation best shows the juxtaposition between nobility and brutality? Why do you think so?

♦ What is the best way to introduce our quotation?

♦ What should we 'zoom in' on in this quotation?

♦ What literary terms would it be useful to mention here?

♦ How can we extend and develop our explanation here?

♦ How will the reader respond to this idea?

♦ What does this show us about Tennyson's message to the reader?

♦ (Once finished.) Have we missed anything out? Could our ideas be explained further?

As the students were answering, I wrote up the paragraph – bit by bit. At times there was disagreement and on one occasion I had to overrule the class when the quotation they had chosen was not suitable. We had a quick class vote: which adjective would work best here – 'violent' or 'savage'?

Now that the class had seen an example, and had watched and participated in the production of another, it was time for independent, silent practice. They wrote a new paragraph on the sixth and final verse of Tennyson's poem, looking at how Tennyson demands that the nobility and heroism of the suicidal soldiers is never forgotten.

Another notable modelling technique is paragraph upscaling. Take a poor paragraph and – as with the sentence escalator – work with the class to improve it. It is an excellent way to show the class how to edit their work.

Over time, you will develop the confidence to improvise – to model on the spot. Instead of preparing a specific model, English teacher Sam Kashmiri likes to improvise by letting her students challenge her with a hard question, which she has to write a response to on the board. She believes that pristine pre-written models hide the difficulty of the writing process, and that it is important to bare your soul as a teacher. If you are struggling, say you are struggling, and in doing so you will model the fact that good writing is never easy.

4. Model Long

How can I find the time to model full texts?

While sentence and paragraph modelling fit neatly into a single lesson, whole-text modelling does not. Whole-text modelling is usually best done through sharing pre-written exemplars. It is also best to avoid using only one example. It is much easier to put your finger on quality when you experience it in comparison. There are two simple ways you can do this:

1   Read through three excellent, but very different, student-written examples and guide your students towards two things: the unique factors that make each stand out and the generic features that unite all three. This works very well when teaching creative writing as it demonstrates that even though there are some unifying features in the best writing, good writers manipulate techniques in individual ways.

2   Read two texts of differing quality side by side. These could be teacher-written or student examples. Then guide your class to explain why the better example is stronger than the weaker example. This process helps to accentuate aspects of quality that are difficult to perceive in single, isolated texts. Think of a tall student and a short student walking through the school gate side by side: the height difference is more starkly apparent – comedic, even! – when they are next to each other than when they are apart.

There are some other very nifty approaches to whole-text modelling. One was shared by head teacher and writer John Tomsett in his book *This Much I Know About Love Over Fear*. He shows his students a well-planned essay and asks them to highlight and "identify the key sentences which, when strung together, will encapsulate the essay's argument".[6] This helps students to see the clarity of design and structure in expert writing.

It is also important to model the key metacognitive processes of writing – planning, monitoring and reviewing – whenever you can. We will explore these in the coming chapters.

Reflective Questions

- ◆ Do you improve students' mental representations of good writing by immersing them in a range of high-quality exemplars?

- ◆ Have your students developed the habit of writing for a target audience so that their writing has greater impact?

- ◆ Do you improve your students' understanding of the processes of writing by modelling sentences, paragraphs and complete texts directly?

---

6 John Tomsett, *This Much I Know About Love Over Fear: Creating a Culture of Truly Great Teaching* [Kindle edn] (Carmarthen: Crown House Publishing, 2015), loc. 852.

Chapter 8

Practising Writing

Harry and the playing field

You have been teaching Harry for six months. At the start of every lesson, he slumps down at his desk and takes an eternity to take his equipment from his bag. Today is no different. By the time he has opened his book, most of his peers have written down the date and title and are halfway through the starter task.

A little later, you set and clearly explain a writing task. Everybody else gets started, pens moving eagerly. But Harry? He's watching the PE lesson out of the window.

You skip over to Harry and talk through the task again. You help him with his first sentence and then you leave him to it. A couple of minutes later you glance back over at him. Lo and behold, he's staring at the playing field again!

By the end of the lesson he has written a single paltry sentence.

I am sure you recognise Harry. We all have those students who seem to exert so much effort in not writing that it would be easier just to get on with the task. Once or twice in my career I have had a whole class full of them. Not only is Harry putting in no effort whatsoever, but he is also throwing away the opportunities available to him to practise his writing.

In 1964, *How Children Fail* by John Holt, an account of how some schoolchildren can slip by the wayside, was first published:

> ... *these children see school almost entirely in terms of the day-to-day and hour-to-hour tasks that we impose on them. This is not at all the way the teacher thinks of it. The conscientious teacher thinks of himself as taking his students (at least part way) on a journey to some glorious destination.*[1]

The problem is not just Harry; it is also the quiet multitudes who scribe away diligently in every lesson, but never really become any better. For them, as Holt observed, writing is a task to complete to get through the day. Somehow we need to help these children transform their conception of writing. It is not just something you do in school: every word you write represents a chance to get better. Work is admin. Practice, on the other hand, has a destination.

In *Making Every Lesson Count*, Shaun Allison and I surveyed the evidence that confirms the crucial role that practice has in learning. To get better at something, we need to practise at the outer reaches of our ability: we need to be set challenging objectives, make a sustained effort to achieve them, listen to the feedback we receive ... and then start on the next goal.

However, this should be counterbalanced with another type of practice: practice for fluency. To learn how to write well, children need to have far more opportunities for attempts than they are usually given. This is known as overlearning. Cognitive scientist Daniel Willingham estimates that, as a rule of thumb, students need at least 20% more practice than they are commonly given.[2]

---

1   John Holt, *How Children Fail* (Harmondsworth: Penguin, 1969), p. 36.
2   Daniel T. Willingham, What Will Improve a Student's Memory? *American Educator* (winter 2008–2009): 17–25. Available at: http://www.aft.org/sites/default/files/periodicals/willingham_0.pdf.

My hunch is that even this is too conservative. Cast your mind back to the last time you taught your class how to use the possessive apostrophe. Did they all get it when you explained it? Did they complete the tasks you set them accurately? I imagine they did. Two weeks later, however, were all students applying the rules accurately? Almost certainly not.

The solution is simple in theory but hard to execute. Children must come to realise that all writing is practice. Writing the date and title, copying down some notes, answering a list of questions, completing grammar drills, annotating a poem, writing a story or completing an analytical essay – they all help to form and solidify writing habits. Practice makes permanent. If a child concentrates on writing tidily, accurately and clearly, and if she rigorously checks and edits her work, her writing will be deliberate and in time will improve. Conversely, if she rushes, regularly loses concentration and cannot be bothered to edit, then these habits will become more and more intractable.

It is also important that students practise the constituent parts of writing as well as writing whole texts. When writing whole texts, a student has to combine a dizzying array of knowledge and skills; it puts huge pressure on working memory and there are a thousand potential hazards on which to run aground. As we have seen, lessons devoted to sentence construction, punctuation rules and spelling rules give students a chance to hone and practise these skills in isolation.

1. Create the Culture

How do I establish and maintain a culture of practice?

Social norms are very important. If we can create a culture of practice it has the potential to become self-sustaining. If everyone else is doing it, most students will become drawn towards this prevailing culture.

We can achieve this through psychological savviness.

♦ **Set the ethos.** From the first time we lay eyes on a class, we must spell out the difference between work completion and purposeful practice. All writing has the potential to strengthen – or weaken – our writing 'muscles'.

♦ **Clear rules and clear sanctions.** Set these at the beginning of the year and stick to them. Should students underline dates and titles? What will happen if careless errors are repeated? What are your rules for paragraphing? How will you respond if standards of handwriting and accuracy slip? If your classroom culture is warm and trusting, then sanctions will work well.

♦ **Benchmark brilliance.** At the start of the academic year, when your class are (hopefully) fresh and eager to please, have all students complete a piece of high-quality writing – perhaps a page of description or critical textual analysis. Give them lots of support and scaffolding and allow time for redrafting. Have the final polished piece placed in a prominent position, such as on the cover of an exercise book. From this moment, insist that all subsequent work aspires to that quality, and if a student starts to doubt himself, use it as a concrete record of his capability.[3]

♦ **Make the bright spots visible.** Share high-quality work wherever possible. Photograph it and project it for everyone to see. Use it to model. Use it to give feedback. Pin it to your walls. Create portfolios of excellent work and have students sift through them. Read exquisite sentences out loud as you are circulating. Show exercise books at parents' evenings.

♦ **Praise them.** Always praise the effort students exert and the processes they employ, rather than the child's innate

---

3   See also my blog post: A Benchmark of Brilliance, *Reflecting English* (5 February 2014). Available at: https://reflectingenglish.wordpress. com/2014/02/05/a-benchmark-of-brilliance/.

ability.[4] "It's great to see how hard everyone is working on their rhetorical techniques today." "Grace, you have used a fantastic adjective here – 'solemn'." Create a ripple effect so that the praise can be heard by other students.

♦ **Nudge them.** The most effective way to change someone's behaviour is by helping them to believe that a certain behaviour is normal. It is usually more effective than trying to convince them to change their attitude.[5] If laziness and bad habits are creeping in, try tactical deception. Praise them, don't berate them:

> *It's great to see how many of you are checking back through your work.*

> *Wow, so many of you are getting your full stops and capital letters 100% accurate.*

> *I love the range of vocabulary I am seeing at the moment!*

If your students are led to believe that everybody else is doing it, the incentive will be to appear normal so they will increase their efforts.

♦ **Never let off.** Spelling, grammar and punctuation accuracy is always important, whatever the task – even if it is just a simple, short-answer quiz. Always insist upon it: good writing habits are easy to break and hard to fix.

These strategies do come with a caveat. If students are practising at the edge of their ability, then mistakes are not only likely but also very useful to you as a teacher. There is a huge difference between thoughtless punctuation errors and a slight miscue when working with a new technique or tricky idea. Ensure that the difference between needless errors and ambitious miscues is made very explicit to the class.

---

4   See Carol Dweck, *Mindset: Changing the Way You Think to Fulfil Your Potential* (London: Robinson, 2012).

5   Cass R. Sunstein and Richard H. Thaler's book, *Nudge: Improving Decisions About Health, Wealth and Happiness* (London: Penguin, 2009), is well worth a read.

2. Go with the Flow

How do I achieve the optimal conditions for writing?

Training the class to write in periods of sustained silence is an imperative for every English teacher. Writing happens at the meeting point between many complex cognitive processes. At any moment the spell can be broken.

This is why children, especially those with poor literacy skills, cannot write well in a room full of distractions. Research into multitasking shows, categorically, that the human mind cannot think about two things at once, and that attempts to do so lead to poorer performance.[6] When Josh turns around mid-sentence to smirk at a whispered comment from Holly, at least two trains of thought are damaged.

It is important to get students into the habit of writing independently and in silence in your classroom. Start this early and be strict about it. It's tough love, English teacher style.

In *The Confident Teacher*, English teacher Alex Quigley refers to the idea of flow, first popularised by Mihaly Csikszentmihalyi.[7] Flow is the feeling of becoming so immersed in a task that the rest of the world feels like it has receded and diminished. In an English classroom, it becomes just you, your thoughts, your pen and your writing – everything else fades away. Quigley writes about how flow can be achieved through confident behaviour management:

The 'flow' is so crucial because it correlates with students maximising their time on task. By creating routine behaviours

---

6   See Pedro de Bruyckere, Paul A. Kirschner and Caspar D. Hulshof, *Urban Myths about Learning and Education* [Kindle edn] (London: Academic Press, 2015), loc. 2248– 2322.

7   Mihaly Csikszentmihalyi, *Flow: The Psychology of Happiness*, rev. edn (London: Rider, 2002).

to maintain 'flow', we achieve a thousand marginal gains of time throughout the school year.[8]

So how can you bring to life a 'silent flow' in your classroom?

♦ **Write regularly.** Most English lessons should include at least ten minutes of silent writing. Concentrate on achieving this first, before you start worrying about how to improve your students' writing.

♦ **Adopt a position.** When you have set up a task and have asked the students to start, find a position where you can see all the students at once – perhaps a corner of the room. Stand still and stand quietly. If anybody entreats you for help, motion them back to their work with a downward hand.

♦ **Map a path.** After a couple of minutes, work out which students need prompting and support. Move between these students swiftly and quietly, as if you are tiptoeing past the room of a sleeping baby. Give them the quickest, simplest advice you can, then return to your corner. Don't move until everybody has got started. You can, unwittingly, become the biggest distractor in the room. A carefully thought-through seating plan can also help with this.

♦ **Retreat or circulate.** When things are going well (or when, quite frankly, you need a break!), leave them to it. Often you can return to your desk. In doing so, you are sending the subliminal message that you are trusting them to work independently. If you choose to circulate, do not allow students to raise their hands. If they do, they will stop writing. Train them to indicate their need by using some other kind of sign – such as a card or a red page in their planner – and to continue with their work whenever possible. That way, they can carry on and you

---

8 Quigley, *The Confident Teacher*, p. 161.

will not disturb the peace by racing from student to student.

♦ **Interrupt wisely.** At times you will need to break the silence – perhaps for praise, for reminders or to address common errors. But do so carefully. Every time you speak you interrupt twenty-five or more thoughts mid-flow.

In sum, the nurturing of silent practice is an art form, a classroom ballet.

All of us can do it, even with the most troublesome of classes. On the day I first drafted this section, my Year 9 class wrote for twenty minutes in silence at the start of the lesson. At the beginning of the year I could barely get them to sit down when they came into the room. Don't give up. It can be done.

3. Scaffold It

How do I support my students to practise at the edge of their ability?

As we have already explored, poorly designed or very open writing tasks can be counterproductive. One of the great skills of the expert English teacher is knowing when to give a class extra writing support and when to remove this support. Again, it is a nuanced process that involves your subject knowledge, your knowledge of individual students and your understanding of the likely misconceptions – the sticking points and mistakes – that a task is likely to present.

The idea of scaffolding is a useful metaphor. When introducing a new skill – from using an apostrophe of omission to planning a sophisticated analytical essay – we should provide adequate support, and then remove the support bit by bit so that the child is given greater independence. Ideally, the scaffolding should mean that each student is working in their struggle zone:

Comfort zone	Struggle zone	Panic zone
Low challenge. Low stress. Limited thinking. Limited learning.	High challenge. Low stress. Thinking required. Effective learning.	Very high challenge. High stress. Cognitive overload. Limited learning.

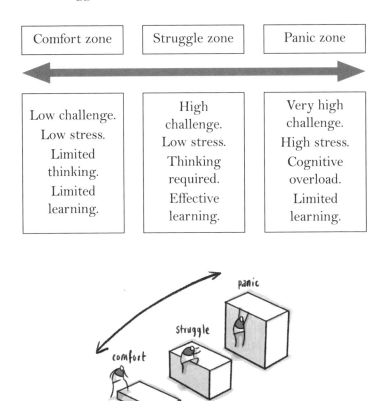

Ask these five questions before planning any writing task:

1 Do I want a long, detailed response or a short, focused response?

2 Am I expecting students to practise writing fluently at speed or slowly and carefully?

3 Will students have a choice of tasks or will they all complete the same one?

4 Is the task designed to practise/test writing skills or to test understanding of a new concept – or both?

5 Are they practising writing whole texts or isolated parts of texts?

Once you have answered these you can choose scaffolding appropriate to the task. Sometimes you will provide this extra support to all students; at other times you will select the few who need it. If scaffolding is for only a small proportion of the class, provide it with discretion. Waltzing over to a student and announcing, in front of her peers, that you have created a little something to help her out can inadvertently communicate your low expectation of her. It is usually best to ask the child whether they would prefer extra help or not: if they would not, monitor them closely and intervene in a subtle way if you need to.

So how can English teachers provide this support?

♦ **Tight parameters.** Remember that very open tasks can lead to decision paralysis and superficial detail.

♦ **Tick-lists.** These can have a transformational effect on learning the processes of writing. If you are teaching paragraph structure, ask the students to check each stage of the paragraph against a tick-list. If you are teaching whole-text structure, ask them to check off each stage of their argument. Or, alternatively, combine the two. A tick-list can also be used to take students through the stages of the editing process.

Tick-lists are less effective when written in subjective language. Compare the statement, "I have used a topic sentence to introduce the main idea of this paragraph" with, "My writing is structured coherently." The first is concrete and meaningful and has a clear direction. The second is a hazy judgement of quality and is unhelpful – unless, of course, you already know how to structure a text coherently.

♦ **Sentence starters and structures.** These have a range of benefits: they provide useful starting cues, they introduce the style and tone to be maintained and, at their best, they provoke deeper thinking. Doug Lemov argues that by providing sentence starters and structures we can promote more rigorous and academic thinking.[9]

Consider how the following starters could be used in a piece of critical evaluation:

◊ The most important word/sentence/idea/chapter/ moment is … because …

◊ Even though …

◊ The reader is caught between … and …

◊ On the surface … but underneath …

◊ In spite of everything, …

◊ At its core …

◊ The most controversial thing about …

Depending on how they are deployed, sentence starters and structures have a dual purpose. They make work more accessible, yet they also promote deeper thinking.[10]

♦ **Key words.** Give your students a list of vocabulary terms that you want them to include in their writing. It's best to

---

9 Doug Lemov, *Teach Like a Champion 2.0: 62 Techniques That Put Students on the Path to College* (San Francisco, CA: Jossey-Bass, 2015), pp. 285–289.

10 For more on this topic see my blog post: Beyond PEE: Reuniting Reading and Writing, *Reflecting English* (21 June 2014). Available at: https://reflectingenglish.wordpress.com/2014/06/21/beyond-pee-reuniting-reading-and-writing/.

limit it to a handful of words, depending on the length of the task. You can also stipulate the order in which you want the words to appear.

I gave my Year 9 class the task of writing a summary of Wilfred Owen's poem 'Futility'. The instructions were: "Write a 50-word summary of 'Futility'. Include the terms 'death', 'sun', 'symbol', 'life', 'faith' and 'existence' in that order. Start with: Wilfred Owen's 'Futility' explores …"

The best responses read like this:

> *Wilfred Owen's 'Futility' explores the death of a young soldier. His comrades move him into the sun, once a symbol of life, in the hope that it will revive him. However, the soldier remains lifeless. By the end of the poem, the narrator has lost all his faith in existence.*

♦ **Discussion.** All forms of discussion – teacher-directed, paired or grouped – are useful scaffolds immediately prior to writing. Make sure your class know that the discussion will lead directly to a subsequent writing task. As always, keep these discussions speedy and highly structured. For example:

> *In three minutes you will be writing a description of your protagonist. You will be showing, not telling. Turn to the person next to you and explain which three things you will describe – perhaps your character's hands, their body movement and the tone of their voice. Remember: you must only talk to the person next to you and I will choose three pairs to respond. Go.*

♦ **Teach a bit, write a bit, teach a bit, write a bit.** Scaffolding extended writing is a tricky business. Early in my career, I would resort to the worst kind of spoon-feeding by handing out double-sided writing frames that would guide the students, sentence by sentence, to the response I wanted. There was no room for any divergence or hard thinking. My students produced work that appeared proficient, yet this papered over the gaps in their learning. Now, if I want to take my students through extended writing stage by stage, I ask them to plan their writing first. Then I model the opening to my own example (in the same genre but always different to the students' task), before I ask the students to write theirs. After this, I model the next part of my exemplar and they complete theirs. And so on, until the piece is finished. Therefore, at each stage the class are supported, yet always encouraged to think hard for themselves.

♦ **Teach them how to plan.** In a sense, a plan is a self-created scaffold. Planning is an essential metacognitive writing skill, and without it the final written product tends to be either too brief or too repetitive. The ultimate goal of all scaffolding tasks, therefore, is to hand planning duties over to the students over time. There are various ways to organise plans – lists and visual–spatial organisers being the most common. There are several parts to planning: generating a range of different ideas, choosing the most relevant and designing a logical sequence. Students also need to understand the notion of the rough plan: they can modify – or even abandon – their original thoughts if need be.

4. Remove the Scaffolds

How do I ensure that scaffolding leads to autonomy, not dependence?

As the aim of scaffolding is always to pass autonomy to the students over time, decisions about the quantity of scaffolding should be taken carefully. Gradual dismantling of scaffolding can take place over the course of one lesson. However, longer-term approaches, like those that follow, are likely to have a more profound impact.

- **Over units.** Let's imagine you are teaching a unit on Shakespeare's *Romeo and Juliet*. Your ultimate aim is that your class will write a timed, hour-long evaluative essay on an aspect of the play. As you read the play, you ask them to complete five to ten minutes of writing at the end of each lesson. In the first few lessons you give them starter sentences to complete – for example, "At the start of the play, Shakespeare creates the inevitability of tragedy by …" As the scheme of work continues, you remove this scaffolding a little – for example, "Choose two quotations from Act 1, Scene 2 to explore how Shakespeare uses religious imagery to describe Romeo and Juliet's love." As you move towards the end of the unit, you switch to more open tasks to complete – for example, "Write a paragraph that sums up how Shakespeare presents the role of fate in the play." By the end of the unit, the class have had enough scaffolding to be ready to write an independent essay under exam conditions.

- **Over a key stage or academic year.** Start the year with more scaffolding so that you can set a high standard. By the end of the year, expect them to write in a similar style, only now with less scaffolding.

- **Over five years.** Work with your department to consider how you will gradually remove scaffolding over five years.

There are times, however, when it is useful to withdraw scaffolding before the students are completely ready. Using some unsupported tasks quite early on can help you to diagnose your students' writing needs. This gives you valuable data to inform your future teaching. You also have a duty to prepare your students psychologically for their final exams: the more they get used to working without scaffolds, the less of a shock those closed-book GCSE exams will be.

Perhaps the most important message of this chapter is this: independent writing is a destination, not a teaching strategy in its own right.

Reflective Questions

♦ Are your students immersed in a culture of purposeful practice, rather than merely 'admin'?

♦ Do your students realise that writing habits – good or bad – become permanent with repetition?

♦ Do you cultivate a culture of silent immersion in extended writing?

♦ Do you develop your students' independence by providing scaffolded direction, and then removing this when the time is right?

Chapter 9
Feedback

Much ado about nothing

Rachel has just spent the last hour writing a formal letter as an exam practice task. She has worked hard in that time. In fact, she has written two-and-a-half sides of A4. The problem is that her writing is littered with errors: no paragraphs, a few randomly positioned full stops, an inconsistent formal register.

Rachel's English teacher, Miss Collins, spends four hours marking the class set in detail – writing three to four sentences of feedback and leaving three targets for each student – and hands the work back a week later. Rachel has worked her socks off. So has Miss Collins. But the problem is that the feedback is ineffective. The next time Rachel writes, she repeats the same mistakes.

Research suggests that good feedback has a significant impact on student learning.[1] Indeed, some English teachers

---

1   See, for example, John Hattie's *Visible Learning: A Synthesis of Over 800 Meta-Analyses Relating to Achievement* (New York: Routledge, 2008) and the Education Endowment Foundation's toolkit: https://educationendowmentfoundation.org.uk/resources/teaching-learning-toolkit/feedback.

believe that marking has a transformational effect. However, others – such as John Wolstenholme – are more sceptical. He stresses that the main purpose of marking should be to praise and acknowledge a student's work, rather than to help a child improve their knowledge and skill.

Surprisingly, at the time of writing, there is scant robust research evidence to support either position.[2] This is why it is so important not to conflate feedback with written marking. Yes, feedback is clearly beneficial, but marking is only one form of feedback – a very inefficient one at that.

Miss Collins' predicament is a common one. A class set of extended writing takes a significant amount of time to read, let alone mark. Unfortunately, feedback is often received after the horse has bolted – too late to rectify mistakes and misconceptions. A solution is to find faster and more efficient ways to give feedback while the work is being completed. Students like Rachel, whose literacy skills are weak, require feedback that guides them as they are working – especially as written comments are easily forgotten.

Another issue is the opportunity cost of marking. Miss Collins' feedback took several hours to complete. Would skimming through the work and using her findings to plan the next few lessons have been a better use of her time? Primary teacher Michael Tidd sees marking as a prime example of the law of diminishing returns: as more investment is made, the overall return on that investment increases, but at a declining rate.[3] The first few moments of reading and commenting on a student's work – our initial investment – give us a good picture of the child's strengths and

---

2   See Victoria Elliott, Jo-Anne Baird, Therese N. Hopfenbeck, Jenni Ingram, Ian Thompson, Natalie Usher, et al., *A Marked Improvement? A Review of the Evidence on Written Marking* (London: Education Endowment Foundation, 2016). Available at: https://educationendowmentfoundation.org.uk/public/files/Publications/EEF_Marking_Review_April_2016.pdf.

3   Michael Tidd, Why We've Got Planning and Marking All Wrong (Part 1), *Ramblings of a Teacher* (5 November 2015). Available at: https://michaelt1979.wordpress.com/2015/11/05/why-weve-got-planning-and-marking-all-wrong-part-1/.

weakness. After that, the investment of time – the handwritten comments and the grading – have less and less impact on learning. The three to four sentences that Miss Collins wrote on Rachel's work proved her dedication to her student, but did they really help Rachel to improve?

Peer feedback is another enticing option to lessen the load. It can be undertaken quickly and within the lesson. However, once again, it is not without its faults. Researcher Graham Nuthall estimated that 80% of the feedback students receive is from their peers – and much of it is wrong![4]

Feedback has four main roles: to show your students what they need to aim for; to keep them on track; to let them know whether they have got there or not; and to point them in the direction of their next goal. It is also important to consider its reciprocal nature: feedback *to* students improves their knowledge and skills; feedback *from* students helps us to plan our teaching more effectively (as shown in the figure below).

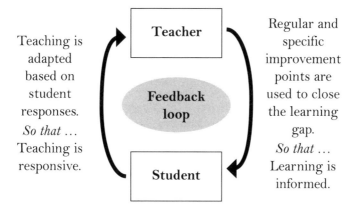

Teaching is adapted based on student responses. *So that …* Teaching is responsive.

Teacher

Feedback loop

Student

Regular and specific improvement points are used to close the learning gap. *So that …* Learning is informed.

---

4   Graham Nuthall, *The Hidden Lives of Learners* (Wellington: New Zealand Council for Educational Research Press, 2007).

A recent Education Endowment Foundation paper summarises the paucity of evidence we have on marking to date and recommends the following:[5]

♦ Careless mistakes should be marked differently to errors resulting from misunderstanding. The latter may be best addressed by providing hints or questions which lead pupils to underlying principles; the former by simply marking the mistake as incorrect, without giving the right answer.

♦ Awarding grades for every piece of work may reduce the impact of marking, particularly if pupils become preoccupied with grades at the expense of a consideration of teachers' formative comments.

♦ The use of targets to make marking as specific and actionable as possible is likely to increase pupil progress.

♦ Pupils are unlikely to benefit from marking unless some time is set aside to enable pupils to consider and respond to marking.

♦ Some forms of marking, including acknowledgement marking, are unlikely to enhance pupil progress. A mantra might be that schools should mark less in terms of the number of pieces of work marked, but mark better.

This chapter will take heed of these recommendations to touch on three areas: how to improve the quality of in-the-moment feedback, how to improve the efficiency and quality of marking and how to improve approaches to peer and self-checking.

---

5 Elliott et al., *A Marked Improvement?*, p. 5.

1. Edit First

How do I get my students to check their work?

One of the side effects of the current obsession with marking in the UK has been to switch the responsibility for reviewing and editing work from the student to the teacher. Learned helplessness can be induced if students are not encouraged to make changes to their work and are allowed to fall back on the knowledge that you will mark every mistake for them.

Nevertheless, creating an editing culture is no easy feat. Many students are motivated by task completion – they will race through their work at breakneck speed, lay down their pens and lean back in their chairs, convinced that they have done what has been asked of them and need do no more. This cycle has to be broken. But how?

♦ **Teach a simple process.** To provide clarity and consistency, you need to choose an editing process that you are going to work with, and stick with it. I like the STAR strategy, first suggested to me by English teacher and blogger Mark Miller,[6] who adapted it from the work of US teacher Kelly Gallagher:

> **Substitute** – replace ineffective words with more suitable replacements.

---

6 Mark Miller, Revision Before Redrafting, *The Goldfish Bowl* (7 December 2013). Available at: http://thegoldfishbowl.edublogs.org/2013/12/07/revision-before-redrafting/.

> **Take things out** – pare down clumsy sentences and remove redundant details.
>
> **Add things in** – give more detail or elaborate ideas in more depth.
>
> **Rearrange** – consider the order of ideas within paragraphs as well as the structure of the whole text.

♦ **Model it.** Take your time to introduce the editing process. First off, model how to use it. Display a piece of student work – or a pre-written exemplar – and 'live model' how to improve it using the STAR editing strategy (or similar) stage by stage. At first, you might decide to leave out the rearrange part (it is quite tricky) but as you move through the year, add it to your students' repertoire.

♦ **Practise it.** Introduce the editing process at the beginning of the year and have your students practise it until it becomes a habit. Before they practise with their own work, give them time to work on exemplars – in pairs and then individually. If you can, introduce it at a department level. Imagine the powerful effect of *all* students editing in the same way for five years, from Year 7 to Year 11.

♦ **Insist upon it.** Find time for students to do it. A resting period between writing and editing can help students to see mistakes and errors with fresh eyes (I certainly needed it for this book!). If you have time, choose a piece of writing from earlier in the year and have students improve that too. Some teachers refuse to mark work if there is no evidence that the students have edited it. Remember that editing presents ripe pickings for praise: "I love the way you have changed that adjective, Emily." As with everything, if you teach it well, and show that you value it, in time most of your students will adopt it.

2. Do It There and Then

How do I give feedback while students are writing?

You are about to take off from London Heathrow on a flight to New York City. Inexplicably, your pilot taxies to the wrong runway and, in a matter of minutes, you are flying towards mainland Europe. The further you fly in the wrong direction, the harder it is for your pilot to undo his mistake.

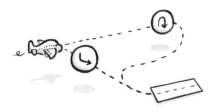

This exemplifies why the provision of regular feedback *during* writing tasks is so important. The further they go off track, the further our students compound the errors and misconceptions they make.

On the flip side, a huge mistake can also provide a valuable salutary lesson. In future, your pilot will pay closer attention to air traffic control commands! The trick, again, is to strike a balance between giving and withholding feedback so that your students have enough room to think for themselves but enough guidance to avoid embedding intractable errors and misconceptions.

Here are a few simple but effective strategies:

♦ **Seating plan.** Those who need lots of quick 'check-ins' should be sat in positions that allow you to give feedback quickly and efficiently. Avoid the far corners of the room or long distances from your desk.

- **Simple praise.** Don't forget that indicating to a child that he is on track is also important. Pointing to an aspect of his work and saying "That's good" might be all it takes.

- **Highlighter action.** As the class are working, move around and highlight spelling and punctuation mistakes they have made. Ask them to correct them immediately.

- **Ask a question.** This can be verbal or written. Your question might be to extend the child's thinking or to help him break down a problem he might have.

- **Give the answer.** Sometimes it is wise to answer the child's question or fill her in on a piece of missing knowledge. For instance, she might ask, "How do I spell Eiffel Tower?" as she is writing a story. The faff created by asking her to look it up or getting her to guess is rarely worth the effort. If, however, you suspect the problem is due to lack of effort or bad study habits, send it back: "Look back to the notes from yesterday – you will find the answer there."

- **Spotlight an example.** Stop the class to read out examples. Even better, use a visualiser or find a way to take a quick photo and display it. This gives the child something concrete to compare her work with and edit accordingly.

- **Back to teaching.** Sometimes it is sensible to stop a whole class as they are working, particularly if a crucial misconception becomes apparent. Individual feedback is very inefficient if the problem relates to the whole class.

Part of the art of teaching is working out what works best for each child. In most cases, the above strategies are enough, but some students present with unique problems that require unique responses. All teachers, even the most experienced, are sometimes presented with students for whom entirely different approaches are required. Use your knowledge of your classes to adapt strategies as appropriate.

3. Mark Light

How can I make my marking more manageable?

Marking is the perennial bugbear of the English teacher. I know teachers who get up at 5 a.m. to slave over books before they come into school; I know other teachers who schedule in coffee-fuelled all-nighters to keep the marking at bay.

However, it does not have to be that way. Lucy Wood, who has been an English teacher for over a decade, hardly ever spends her evenings and weekends marking, and yet the quality of work in her students' books is astonishing. And even more astonishing is the fact that the work has been marked.

How does Lucy do it? First, if you are awarding a mark or a grade, do not waste time procrastinating – go with your gut instinct. Second, avoid the temptation to mark everything. Only mark the key thing you feel that the student needs to get better at. Keep it simple and keep it razor sharp.

Experienced teachers have a wealth of cunning manoeuvres up their sleeves. Here are a few I have picked up over the years.

Use codes	Create a list of common successes and targets. Rather than writing them out in full over and over again in students' books, simply leave a code (e.g. S3 and T2). Present the key on the board and have each student write in the corresponding comment.
Use tick-sheets	Print out your lists of successes and targets as a tick-list. Simply tick those that apply for that student.
Circle errors	If a child has made a spelling or punctuation mistake, just circle it. Circle no more than four or five in every piece of work, irrespective of the number of mistakes. Expect them to edit their mistakes. If you feel that the child will not understand, give them a clue (e.g. 'exag_____' for exaggerate).
Write sparingly	If you like personal comments, keep them concise and combine with codes. "Jess, I'm so thrilled about the improvements you have made in this piece. Keep up the hard work!" becomes "Fantastic improvement, Jess! – S2". Remember, personal comments can be more meaningful when delivered verbally.

One pen	Some schools suggest using different coloured pens for different types of marking. All that switching between pens adds up to a huge amount of time. One pen is more than enough.
No sheets	Some schools expect teachers to write feedback on separate sheets to hand back with the work. This is pointless and a sure-fire way to slow down marking and increase workload.
Open books	Ask students to hand in their books open on the first page you will mark – you will shave off ten minutes per class set.
Gist read	You do not need to mark every word of an extended piece of writing. Read the first paragraph in detail, work out the student's main area for improvement (like Lucy Wood does) and skim-read the rest, concentrating on the improvement area whenever it comes up.
Use peers	There are dangers to peer marking. However, if you check the peer marking, you can write a simple, "I agree". You can overrule anything inaccurate.
Return it quickly	Students usually appreciate this more than extra detail.
Examples as feedback	Rather than writing extended comments, show your class examples of the best work produced. This avoids the abstract language in which most marking rubrics are written.

At Michaela Free School in London, English teachers have created a system that completely bypasses the marking of individual books, yet allows teachers to read work more frequently, celebrate successes and share improvement tips. Teachers read through the class's work, looking for general strengths and weaknesses. The feedback session will begin with students working through general spelling mistakes, then move on to reading out a list of those who have been successful and less successful, before looking closely at the positive things the teacher has found. Finally, there may well be re-teaching of a common area of weakness. In other words, lots of very regular feedback, but little conventional marking.[7]

Some schools are also devising ingenious feedback systems that bypass the need for marking. In these schools, teachers read the work and fill in a feedback document noting areas of success, notable pieces of work, common knowledge gaps and frequent spelling, punctuation and grammar mistakes. The document is printed out for all students who stick it in their exercise books and highlight the feedback that is pertinent to them. They then get on with the important bit: improving their work.

Whether you believe in marking every book in red pen or not, whether you are obliged to follow a school-wide marking policy or not, it is vital to develop a manageable system. Like all teachers, you need time to plan and research lessons. You need time to switch off too. English teachers must work together to remove the tyranny of foolhardy and highly prescriptive marking expectations.

---

7   See Jo Facer, Marking is Futile, in Katharine Birbalsingh (ed.), *Battle Hymn of the Tiger Teachers: The Michaela Way* (Woodbridge: John Catt Educational, 2016), pp. 46–53.

4. Use Questions

How do I encourage my students to think hard about my feedback?

If one of the purposes of feedback is to alert students to their errors, another is to provoke further thinking. While descriptive advice ("Vary the way you start this sentence.") is useful, we also need students to be thinking for themselves. Metacognition – the awareness of one's own thought processes – is a powerful aspect of learning. This is why questions are such a useful form of feedback; they prompt students to think about their work, in the hope that, eventually, they will internalise these kinds of prompts for themselves.

Let's say you are marking a set of papers on John Steinbeck's *Of Mice and Men*. You want your students to get better at analysing Steinbeck's word choices, evaluating Steinbeck's attitudes and opinions, and making links between the text and the social context.

Focusing on a section of text on the character Slim, you might ask these kinds of questions:

Q1: What are the connotations of the word 'majesty'? What does it suggest about Slim?

Q2: Which of Steinbeck's adjectives best sums up Slim's character?

Q3: How does Steinbeck encourage the reader to admire Slim?

Q4: What does Steinbeck's characterisation of Slim reveal about different forms of authority?

Q5: How has Steinbeck used language to show the contrasting sides of Slim's character?

Q6: What qualities does Slim have that make him unusual for a 1930s ranch-worker?

It is worthwhile to skim-read a cross-section of your class's
books before you write up the questions. That way, you can
use question codes in place of handwritten comments. If
you scaffold the questions at different levels – compare Q1
and Q3, for instance – then it is a neat way to differentiate
your feedback.

You can also devise a list of generic feedback questions (see
the list below for some examples). These can be used by
teachers and peers to annotate work. The game changer here
is to get the students so habitualised to the questions that
they start asking them of their own work.

♦ What would be a more unusual or powerful alternative
  word?

♦ What could you do to make this phrase/sentence more
  formal?

♦ How could you improve the accuracy and grammar of
  this sentence?

♦ How could you avoid being too repetitive in this
  section?

♦ How could you start this sentence in a more interesting
  way?

♦ How could you use a sensory description to bring this
  character/setting alive for the reader?

♦ How could you use figurative language to help the reader
  to visualise it?

♦ How could you use a more imaginative description/sen-
  tence/phrase here?

♦ How could you vary your sentence structures to make
  this part more lively?

♦ What unnecessary detail could you remove from this
  section?

- How could you change the order of this part to make it more gripping for the reader?

- How could you encourage your reader to feel (insert emotion) here?

- What do you need to do to ensure you stay in the same tense?

- How could you surprise the reader here?

- How could you make this part more concise?

- How might you make this section more detailed?

- How could you *show* this rather than *tell* this?

- Could you eavesdrop on your character's thoughts at this point?

- What would be the one thing that would make this sentence even more effective?

- What would be the one thing that would make this paragraph even more effective?

- What would be the one thing that would make this whole piece even more effective?

5. Expect a Response

How do I get my students to best respond to my marking?

Educationalist Dylan Wiliam writes: "The first fundamental principle of effective classroom feedback is that feedback should be more work for the recipient than the donor."[8] This principle is never more true than it is for English teachers. If you are going to mark a set of books or papers, you should ensure that there is time for your class to respond. Since 2012, DIRT (Dedicated Improvement and Reflection Time, which originally appeared in Jackie Beere's *The Perfect (Ofsted) Lesson*[9]) has totally transformed marking in many schools. If you are not familiar with this acronym, it is a very simple concept: ring-fence some time for students to do something in response to your marking.

Always start by asking your students to correct their spelling, punctuation and grammar mistakes. I usually target

---

8   Dylan Wiliam, *Embedded Formative Assessment* [Kindle edn] (Bloomington, IN: Solution Tree Press, 2011), loc. 2635.

9   Jackie Beere, *The Perfect (Ofsted) Lesson*, rev. edn (Carmarthen: Independent Thinking Press, 2012), p. 29.

about five in each student's work. A coding system like this works well:

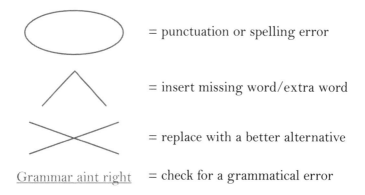

= punctuation or spelling error

= insert missing word/extra word

= replace with a better alternative

Grammar aint right = check for a grammatical error

Ask them to use a different coloured pen to correct their mistakes, to make them accountable, and to write out correct spellings in the margin. I also insist that they do this in silence at first – they must learn to find their own mistakes. Only when they have corrected what they can are they allowed to ask for help from me or a peer.

What you do next might depend on how much time you have and how well the class have completed the original task. You could:

♦ Ask the students to answer any extension questions you have asked, in full sentences.

♦ Show and discuss a good example from a member of the class and have the students edit their own piece in light of this.

♦ Instigate a 'live writing' session which helps you to explain the mistakes the students have made and how to rectify them.

♦ Ask the students to redraft a paragraph according to any targets or advice given – with sentence starters or other scaffolds as a guide.

♦ Ask the students to redraft the complete piece.

♦ Ask the students to complete a different task which allows them to work on targets and advice in a new context.

♦ Ask a student to complete an extension task because they have mastered the original knowledge and skills.

Try to avoid setting a completely different task for each child as this can be hard to manage. If possible, stick to no more than three.

These tasks allow the students to reflect on how they have gone wrong and give them an immediate chance to rectify the mistake. They also allow for careful reflection and help to normalise your culture of practice: when we get things wrong, we put them right. Consider, too, the types of targets you use: are they *feedback* targets that provide guidance towards the improvement of the piece of work you have just marked? Or are they *feed-forward* targets that can be carried on to the next topic you are to teach? Or both?

Redrafting is a vital constituent of real-world writing. No newspaper article or book goes to press without undergoing a demanding editing process. No job application or letter to a client should be sent without several rounds of checking. It is a habit best formed at school. Nevertheless, the fact that a child has improved their work as a result of your marking should not be mistaken as strong evidence of learning. A beautifully polished redraft may look good stuck into an exercise book; it may even bring a student pride and an improved sense of self-efficacy. However, unless this standard of work can be repeated independently, it is not a true reflection of capability. Indeed, it is a better measure of the time and effort you have put into the marking, rather than the student's learning. The idea that DIRT always neatly closes the gap is enticing but often flawed.

As John Wolstenholme puts it, you can't teach a student how to use a semicolon by writing "use a semicolon" in their book. Feedback is a very flimsy tool for teaching new concepts. When students do not know or understand something, they need to be taught it. Once again, feedback is no panacea.

And, finally, there is nothing as important or as powerful as reading your students' work. It should inform many of your decisions. Red pen or no red pen, DIRT or no DIRT, finding out where your students are, working out where they need to go and then taking them there is the lifeblood of great English teaching. Reflection, adaption and response are absolutely crucial to the success of your students.

Final Thoughts

This book has suggested a wide range of effective English teaching strategies and, as such, has been written to act as a catalyst for future thought and action. The strategies are yours to adapt and improve. Only you are the expert in your classroom. Remember that.

I truly believe that these ideas can lead to better teaching and better learning in English lessons. They belong to a huge body of wisdom and evidence that our profession has accumulated over generations; the exciting thing is that your classroom practice can draw from this and enrich it further. Please share the best ideas from this book as widely as you can and challenge any that you find to be ineffective or superficial.

I have written this book after a decade of English teaching and I still feel like an imposter. There is always so much to learn! The notion that there are such people as outstanding English teachers or such things as perfect English lessons is a pernicious myth. In the final pages of *The Confident Teacher*, Alex Quigley recommends that we should aim to become "the best version of ourselves".[1] Only then can we achieve great things. If we accept that there will always be some teaching problems for which there are no easy solutions and some students for whom the greatest teaching is still not enough, we can become happier and more confident. This is not about giving up, but instead a reasonable acceptance of the limits of our powers.

You should also try to resist the temptation to shoehorn everything from this book into your classroom. Perhaps take the strategies from one chapter – or three strategies from across the book – and attend to those first. Try them out, evaluate the impact and improve upon them. Whenever you

---

1 Quigley, *The Confident Teacher*, p. 282.

are incorporating new ideas, you must also be prepared to streamline. What will you leave out to make room for the new?

And finally. There is much that this book has not touched on. Every day, you have thousands of interactions with young people, all of which have an immeasurable impact on their learning, their well-being and their love – or otherwise! – for our wonderful subject. Remember to direct, remember to immerse and remember to develop lifelong reading and writing habits.

It is the fine details which will allow you to make every English lesson count.

Bibliography

Allison, Shaun and Andy Tharby (2015). *Making Every Lesson Count: Six Principles to Support Great Teaching and Learning* (Carmarthen: Crown House Publishing).

Asbury, Kathryn and Robert Plomin (2013). *G is for Genes: The Impact of Genetics on Education and Achievement* (Chichester: John Wiley).

Beck, Isabel L., Margaret G. McKeown and Linda Kucan (2002). *Bringing Words to Life: Robust Vocabulary Instruction* (New York: Guilford Press).

Beere, Jackie (2012). *The Perfect (Ofsted) Lesson*, rev. edn (Carmarthen: Independent Thinking Press).

Berger, Ron (2003). *An Ethic of Excellence: Building a Culture of Craftsmanship with Students* (Portsmouth, NH: Heinemann).

Bourdieu, Pierre and Jean-Claude Passeron (1977). *Reproduction in Education, Society and Culture*, tr. Richard Nice (London: SAGE).

Christodoulou, Daisy (2013). The Adverb Problem, *The Wing to Heaven* (24 November). Available at: https://thewingtoheaven.wordpress.com/2013/11/24/the-adverb-problem/.

Christodoulou, Daisy (2014). *Seven Myths About Education* (Abingdon: Routledge).

Clark, Ruth C., Frank Nguyen and John Sweller (2006). *Efficiency in Learning: Evidence-Based Guidelines to Manage Cognitive Load* (San Francisco, CA: Pfeiffer).

Coe, Robert (2013). Improving Education: A Triumph of Hope Over Experience. Inaugural lecture, Durham University, 18 June. Available at: http://www.cem.org/attachments/publications/ImprovingEducation2013.pdf.

Coe, Robert, Cesare Aloisi, Steve Higgins and Lee Elliott Major (2014). *What Makes Great Teaching? Review of the Underpinning Research*. Project Report (London: Sutton Trust). Available at: http://www.suttontrust.com/wp-content/uploads/2014/10/What-makes-great-teaching-FINAL-4.11.14.pdf.

Conan Doyle, Arthur (2016 [1892]). 'The Adventure of the Speckled Band', in *The Adventures of Sherlock Holmes* (Ballingslöv: Wisehouse), pp. 123–140.

Curtis, Chris (2014). Death to Sentence Stems! Long Live the Sentence Structures! *Learning From My Mistakes: An English Teacher's Blog* (1 February). Available at: http://learningfrommymistakesenglish.blogspot.co.uk/2014/02/death-to-sentence-stems-long-live.html.

Csikszentmihalyi, Mihaly (2002). *Flow: The Psychology of Happiness*, rev. edn (London: Rider).

de Bruyckere, Pedro, Paul A. Kirschner and Caspar D. Hulshof (2015). *Urban Myths About Learning and Education* [Kindle edn] (London: Academic Press).

Deans for Impact (2015). *The Science of Learning* (Austin, TX: Deans for Impact). Available at: http://deansforimpact.org/pdfs/ The_Science_of_Learning.pdf.

Dickens, Charles (1993 [1843]). *A Christmas Carol* (Ware: Wordsworth Editions).

Didau, David (2014). *The Secret of Literacy: Making the Implicit Explicit* (Carmarthen: Independent Thinking Press).

Didau, David and Nick Rose (2016). *What Every Teacher Needs to Know About Psychology* [Kindle edn] (Woodbridge: John Catt Educational).

Dunlosky, John, Katherine A. Rawson, Elizabeth J. Marsh, Mitchell J. Nathan and Daniel T. Willingham (2013). Improving Students' Learning with Effective Learning Techniques: Promising Directions from Cognitive and Educational Psychology, *Psychological Science in the Public Interest* 14(1): 4–58. Available at: http://www.indiana.edu/~pcl/ rgoldsto/courses/dunloskyimprovinglearning.pdf.

Dweck, Carol (2012). *Mindset: Changing the Way You Think to Fulfil Your Potential* (London: Robinson).

Elliott, Victoria, Jo-Anne Baird, Therese N. Hopfenbeck, Jenni Ingram, Ian Thompson, Natalie Usher, Mae Zantout, James Richardson and Robbie Coleman. (2016). *A Marked improvement? A Review of the Evidence on Written Marking* (London: Education Endowment Foundation). Available at: https://educationendowmentfoundation.org.uk/public/ files/Publications/EEF_Marking_Review_April_2016.pdf.

Ericsson, K. Anders and Robert Pool (2016). *Peak: Secrets from the New Science of Expertise* (New York: Houghton Mifflin).

Facer, Jo (2016). Marking is Futile, in Katharine Birbalsingh (ed.), *Battle Hymn of the Tiger Teachers: The Michaela Way* (Woodbridge: John Catt Educational), pp. 46–53.

Forsyth, Mark (2016). *The Elements of Eloquence: How to Turn the Perfect English Phrase* (London: Icon Books).

Hattie, John (2008). *Visible Learning: A Synthesis of Over 800 Meta-Analyses Relating to Achievement* (New York: Routledge).

Haught-Tromp, Catrinel (2016). The Green Eggs and Ham Hypothesis: How Constraints Facilitate Creativity, *Psychology of Aesthetics, Creativity, and the Arts*. Available at: http://www.rider.edu/sites/default/files/docs/ tromp_haught-tromp_PACA_2016.pdf.

Heath, Chip and Dan Heath (2007). *Made to Stick: Why Some Ideas Take Hold and Others Come Unstuck* (London: Arrow Books).

Heath, Chip and Dan Heath (2011). *Switch: How to Change When Change Is Hard* (London: Random House).

Hirsch, E. D. (2007). *The Knowledge Deficit: Closing the Shocking Education Gap for American Children* (New York: Houghton Mifflin).

Hirsch, E. D. (2016). *Why Knowledge Matters: Rescuing Our Children from Failed Educational Theories* (Cambridge, MA: Harvard Education Press).

Holt, John (1969). *How Children Fail* (Harmondsworth: Penguin).

Institute of Education (2014). Reading for Pleasure, and Attainment in Maths, Vocabulary and Spelling. Research Briefing No. 106. Available at: http://eprints.ioe.ac.uk/18836/1/RB106_Reading_for_Pleasure_Sullivan.pdf.

Kahneman, Daniel (2011). *Thinking, Fast and Slow* [Kindle edn] (London: Allen Lane).

Kirby, Joe (2015). Knowledge Organisers, *Pragmatic Education* (28 March). Available at: https://pragmaticreform.wordpress.com/2015/03/28/knowledge-organisers/.

Leith, Sam (2012). *You Talkin' to Me? Rhetoric from Aristotle to Obama* (London: Profile Books).

Lemov, Doug (2015). *Teach Like a Champion 2.0: 62 Techniques That Put Students on the Path to College* (San Francisco, CA: Jossey-Bass).

Lemov, Doug, Colleen Driggs and Erica Woolway (2016). *Reading Reconsidered: A Practical Guide to Rigorous Literacy Instruction* (San Francisco, CA: Jossey-Bass).

Marzano, Robert J. (2004). *Building Background Knowledge for Academic Achievement: Research on What Works in Schools* (Alexandria, VA: Association for Supervision and Curriculum Development).

Miller, Mark (2013). Revision Before Redrafting, *The Goldfish Bowl* (7 December). Available at: http://thegoldfishbowl.edublogs.org/2013/12/07/revision-before-redrafting/.

Nuthall, Graham (2007). *The Hidden Lives of Learners* (Wellington: New Zealand Council for Educational Research Press).

Oakeshott, Michael (1962). The Voice of Poetry in the Conversation of Mankind, in *Rationalism in Politics and Other Essays* (London: Methuen), pp. 197–247.

Peat, Alan (2008). *Writing Exciting Sentences: Age 7+* (Biddulph: Creative Educational Press).

Quigley, Alex (2016). *The Confident Teacher: Developing Successful Habits of Mind, Body and Pedagogy* (Abingdon: Routledge).

Rigney, Daniel (2010). *The Matthew Effect: How Advantage Begets Further Advantage* (New York and Chichester: Columbia University Press).

Rosenshine, Barak (2012). Principles of Instruction: Research-Based Strategies That All Teachers Should Know, *American Educator* (spring): 12–19. Available at: https://www.aft.org/sites/default/files/periodicals/Rosenshine.pdf.

Stock, Phil (2016). 'Without Contraries There Is No Progression': Or 7 Principles for Pairing Words with Images, *Must Do Better* ... (12 June). Available at: https://joeybagstock.wordpress.com/2016/06/12/without-contraries-there-is-no-progression-or-7-principles-for-pairing-words-with-images/.

Sunstein, Cass R. and Richard H. Thaler (2009). *Nudge: Improving Decisions About Health, Wealth and Happiness* (London: Penguin).

Tharby, Andy (2014). A Benchmark of Brilliance, *Reflecting English* (5 February). Available at: https://reflectingenglish.wordpress.com/2014/02/05/a-benchmark-of-brilliance/.

Tharby, Andy (2014). Beyond PEE: Reuniting Reading and Writing, *Reflecting English* (21 June). Available at: https://reflectingenglish.wordpress.com/2014/06/21/beyond-pee-reuniting-reading-and-writing/.

Tharby, Andy (2016). Question Templates – An Approach to Improving Analysis, *Reflecting English* (2 September). Available at: https://reflectingenglish.wordpress.com/2016/09/02/question-templates-an-approach-to-improving-analysis/.

Tidd, Michael (2015). Why We've Got Planning and Marking All Wrong (Part 1), *Ramblings of a Teacher* (5 November). Available at: https://michaelt1979.wordpress.com/2015/11/05/why-weve-got-planning-and-marking-all-wrong-part-1/.

Tomsett, John (2015). *This Much I Know About Love Over Fear: Creating a Culture of Truly Great Teaching* [Kindle edn] (Carmarthen: Crown House Publishing).

Wiliam, Dylan (2011). *Embedded Formative Assessment* [Kindle edn] (Bloomington, IN: Solution Tree Press).

Willingham, Daniel T. (2007). Critical Thinking: Why Is It So Hard to Teach? *American Educator* (summer): 8–19. Available at: http://www.aft.org/sites/default/files/periodicals/Crit_Thinking.pdf.

Willingham, Daniel T. (2008–2009). What Will Improve a Student's Memory? *American Educator* (winter): 17–25. Available at: http://www.aft.org/sites/default/files/periodicals/willingham_0.pdf.

Willingham, Daniel T. (2009). *Why Don't Students Like School? A Cognitive Scientist Answers Questions About How the Mind Works and What It Means for the Classroom* (San Francisco, CA: Jossey-Bass).

Willingham, Daniel (2012). School Time, Knowledge, and Reading Comprehension, *Daniel Willingham: Science and Education Blog* (7 March). Available at: http://www.danielwillingham.com/daniel-willingham-science-and-education-blog/school-time-knowledge-and-reading-comprehension.

Willingham, Daniel T. (2015). *Raising Kids Who Read: What Parents and Teachers Can Do* (San Francisco, CA: Jossey-Bass).

Making Every Science Lesson Count

Six principles to support great science teaching

Shaun Allison

ISBN: 978-178583182-9

Making Every Science Lesson Count goes in search of answers to the fundamental question that all science teachers must ask: "What can I do to help my students become the scientists of the future?"

Shaun points a sceptical finger at the fashions and myths that have pervaded science teaching over the past decade or so and presents a range of tools and techniques that will help science teachers make abstract ideas more concrete and practical demonstrations more meaningful.

Making Every MFL Lesson Count

Six principles to support great foreign language teaching

James A. Maxwell

ISBN: 978-178583396-0

Making Every MFL Lesson Count equips modern foreign language (MFL) teachers with practical techniques designed to enhance their students' linguistic awareness and to help them transfer the target language into long-term memory.

Written for new and experienced practitioners alike, *Making Every MFL Lesson Count* skilfully marries evidence-based practice with collective experience and, in doing so, inspires a challenging approach to secondary school MFL teaching.

Making Every Primary Lesson Count

Six principles to support great teaching and learning

Jo Payne and Mel Scott

ISBN: 978-178583181-2

Shares a host of strategies designed to cultivate a growth mindset in the primary school classroom and guide children towards independence: motivating both teachers and pupils to aim high and put in the effort required to be successful in all subject areas.

Jo and Mel also offer tips on how to implement effective routines and procedures so that students are clear about what is expected from them.

Making Every Maths Lesson Count

Six principles to support great maths teaching

Emma McCrea

ISBN: 978-178583332-8

Making Every Maths Lesson Count provides practical solutions to perennial problems and inspires a rich, challenging and evidence-based approach to secondary school maths teaching.

Emma shares gimmick-free advice that combines the time-honoured wisdom of excellent maths teachers with the most useful evidence from cognitive science – enabling educators to improve their students' conceptual understanding of maths over time.

Making Every History Lesson Count

Six principles to support great history teaching

Chris Runeckles

ISBN: 978-178583336-6

Writing in the practical, engaging style of the award-winning *Making Every Lesson Count*, Chris Runeckles articulates the fundamentals of great history teaching and shares simple, realistic strategies designed to deliver memorable lessons.

The book is underpinned by six pedagogical principles – challenge, explanation, modelling, practice, feedback and questioning – and equips history teachers with the tools and techniques to help students better engage with the subject matter and develop more sophisticated historical analysis and arguments.

Making Every Geography Lesson Count

Six principles to support great geography teaching

Mark Enser

ISBN: 978-178583339-7

Maps out the key elements of effective geography teaching to help teachers ensure that their students leave their lessons with an improved knowledge of the world, a better understanding of how it works and the geographical skills to support their understanding.

Mark offers an inspiring alternative to restrictive Ofsted-driven definitions of great teaching, and empowers geography teachers to deliver great lessons and celebrate high-quality practice.

Making Every Lesson Count

Six principles to support great teaching and learning

Shaun Allison and Andy Tharby

ISBN: 978-184590973-4

This award-winning title has now inspired a whole series of books. Each of the books in the series are held together by six pedagogical principles – challenge, explanation, modelling, practice, feedback and questioning – and provide simple, realistic strategies that teachers can use to develop the teaching and learning in their classrooms.

A toolkit of techniques that teachers can use every lesson to make that lesson count. No gimmicky teaching – just high-impact and focused teaching that results in great learning, every lesson, every day.

Suitable for all teachers – including trainee teachers, NQTs and experienced teachers – who want quick and easy ways to enhance their practice.

ERA Educational Book Award winner 2016. Judges' comments: "A highly practical and interesting resource with loads of information and uses to support and inspire teachers of all levels of experience. An essential staffroom book."